The Napoleonic Campaign of 1805

NAPOLEON BONAPARTE

The Napoleonic Campaign of 1805

Ulm, Austerlitz and the Campaign in Italy and the Tyrol

ILLUSTRATED

F. W. O. Maycock

LEONAUR

The Napoleonic Campaign of 1805
Ulm, Austerlitz and the Campaign in Italy and the Tyrol
by F. W. O. Maycock

ILLUSTRATED

First published under the title
The Napoleonic Campaign of 1805

Leonaur is an imprint of Oakpast Ltd

Copyright in this form © 2020 Oakpast Ltd

ISBN: 978-1-78282-938-6 (hardcover)
ISBN: 978-1-78282-939-3 (softcover)

http://www.leonaur.com

Publisher's Notes

Contents

Preface

It is hoped that this little book, which lays no claim, to originality but is merely compiled from various authentic sources, may be of some use to my brother officers reading for the Promotion Examinations, and to others interested in Military History.

The brilliant offensive Campaign of 1805, which ended in the overthrow of the Austrian and Russian Armies and the downfall of the Third Coalition, showed the military genius of the Great Emperor at its zenith. His strategy and tactics were alike masterly, and Austerlitz will always rank as one of the most perfect examples of a carefully prepared offensive-defensive battle carried out in absolute accordance with the plans of the commander.

To us, as a nation, the Campaign is especially interesting from the fact that the *Grande Armée*, the most perfectly-trained fighting machine which had yet appeared in Europe, had been organised for the invasion of England.

The various authorities differ considerably in the spelling of the names of persons and places; for the sake of uniformity the latter have been spelt as they appear in the latest edition of the *Harmsworth Atlas and Gazetteer*.

F. W. O. Maycock.

The Barracks.
Bury St. Edmunds.10th April, 1913.

CHAPTER 1

Plans of the Campaign

(1) Causes Rendering the Campaign Inevitable—Pitt's Efforts to Form the Third Coalition—His Difficulties with Russia, Austria, and Prussia.

(2) The Allies' Divergent Objects—Their Plan of Campaign—The Strength and Disposition of their Forces.

(3) Napoleon's Plans—The "Grand Army"—Topography of the Theatre of War.

(1) Shortly after the recommencement of hostilities in May, 1803, Napoleon issued orders for the assembly of a force of 150,000 men for his projected invasion of England, and, stationed in cantonments on the shores of the Channel, they were held in readiness for immediate embarkation.

Besides the resources of France and her feudatories, the Batavian, Cisalpine, and Helvetian Republics, over which he had complete control, Napoleon, by his Treaty with Spain, secured the assistance of her fleet in the struggle for the command of the sea, in which he was about to engage.

In May, 1804, the Addington Ministry fell, and Pitt again came into office. He at once set himself to form a Coalition of the Great Powers, which, by forcing Napoleon to employ his army against his Continental opponents, should remove the menace of invasion from the shores of England,

The "Great Commoner's" task was one of almost insurmountable difficulty, as even the negotiations with Russia, which at first progressed smoothly, were complicated by the question of the disposal of Malta.

Austria, crippled by her long and costly struggle against the French Republic was loath to recommence hostilities, and was, moreover, engaged in the reorganisation of her forces, which would not be completed until the following year. She also clearly foresaw that unless Prussia joined the Coalition she would, as had been the case of latter years, have to bear the brunt of the French onslaught.

The weak and vacillating Frederick William of Prussia was a source of the greatest anxiety to Pitt, for though his powerful and well-trained army would have been invaluable to the Allies, his policy was so shifty that reliance on his co-operation was impossible.

At one time it almost seemed that all Pitt's exertions would be in vain, but Napoleon himself, by his actions in Northern Italy during the summer of 1805, rendered the coalition inevitable. The latter caused himself to be crowned as King of Lombardy at Milan on the 26th of May, and on the 4th of June annexed Genoa to the French Republic, thereby thoroughly alarming Austria and exasperating the *Czar* of Russia. Seeing that Napoleon's ambitions were insatiable, Austria reluctantly entered into an alliance with Russia at the beginning of August, 1805, to which Great Britain immediately gave her adherence. Frederick William, however, coveting Hanover, which had been occupied by the French and which he hoped he might obtain as the price of his neutrality, still refused to join the Allies, in spite of the strong war party at Berlin and the pressure brought to bear on him by the *Czar* of Russia.

(2) Pitt had originally hoped that the Allies would be able to put over half a million men into the field, and, even without the aid of Prussia, the forces of the Coalition amounted, on paper, to the formidable total of over 400,000, the bulk of whom it was hoped would be ready to commence operations by the end of October.

The British Parliament had voted a credit of £5,000,000 to be expended in subsidies to the Allies, but on the definite refusal of Prussia to join the Coalition, the sum was reduced to £3,500,000.

Austria was to furnish a contingent of 250,000 men, Russia 180,000, and the remainder was to be made up of the troops of Great Britain, Sweden, Sardinia and Naples, but the inherent weakness of all coalitions at once became manifest: Austria wished to recover her Italian provinces, Great Britain was anxious to drive the French out of Hanover and free Holland, while the *Czar* insisted on an Anglo-Russian expedition to Southern Italy. It was eventually decided that the Archduke Charles should assume the offensive in Northern Italy with 150,000 men, while 60,000 Austrians and 90,000 Russians, under a Russian commander, should operate in the Valley of the Danube. To connect these two main forces the Archduke John was to hold the Tyrol, while a contingent of 40,000 British, Russians and Swedes was to reconquer Hanover and invade Holland, besides which a force of British, Russians and Neapolitans was to make a diversion in Southern Italy.

Once again, the Allies were committing their former error of dispersing their forces, and the situation was further complicated by the jealousies between the Austrian and Russian commanders, a legacy of their unsuccessful combined operations at the close of the last campaign, brought about to a great extent by the interference of the Aulic Council.

(3) Napoleon was fully aware of the result of Pitt's activity, but, despising the dilatory methods of the Coalition he hoped, if he could only obtain temporary command of the Channel, to complete his conquest of England ere he turned against his opponents on the Continent.

However, when the failure of his admirals to carry out his combinations showed him that his scheme was impossible and he made up his mind to strike at the gathering forces of his opponents, he made his plans with all his habitual vigour and simplicity. Faced by an overwhelming preponderance of numbers and menaced from several quarters at once, he determined to concentrate his forces, fall swiftly on his nearest adversary and crush him, ignoring for the time being the operations in the subsidiary theatres. He decided on advancing from the Rhine and the Main to attack the Austrians in the Valley of the Danube before they could be joined by their Muscovite Allies, while Massena, probably the most able of his lieutenants, contained the

Archduke Charles in Northern Italy until the operations in the main theatre of war made themselves felt.

By this means he would be numerically superior at the critical point, and Massena's force would be fulfilling the true role of a detachment, by neutralising a far superior force of the enemy.

Time, that all-important factor in all military operations, was in his favour, for he could be on the Danube long before the Russians—owing to the immense distances which they had to traverse—could join their Austrian allies, and he confidently counted on dealing his opponents a staggering blow before they could complete their concentration or their minor expeditions produce any appreciable effect.

The army which he was about to lead to such decisive triumphs was undoubtedly the finest fighting machine that had yet appeared in Europe, and had been most carefully reorganised since the previous campaign.

For nearly two years it had been concentrated in cantonments on the shores of the Channel, and steadily trained for war under the leaders who were destined to lead it in the field.

It was divided into corps of from 20,000 to 30,000 strong, each containing an adequate proportion of cavalry and artillery, under the command of his most able marshals, who were given a free hand in the training, administration and interior economy bf their commands.

Consequently, at the outbreak of hostilities, everything from the very first worked smoothly; brigades and divisions found themselves under their accustomed leaders, under whose supervision they had carried out their training. Almost all the officers and non-commissioned officers had already proved their worth in the field, while fully fifty *per cent*, of the rank and file were veterans of the Republican Campaigns.

In addition to the Guard, which as the *corps d'elite* was recruited from the pick of the line regiments, a splendid corps of 8,000 carefully selected grenadiers had been formed by Oudinot and carefully trained by him during the previous winter. The whole army was full of enthusiasm, and eagerly looked forward to adding to its laurels during the ensuing campaign, in which it would

ARCHDUKE CHARLES, DUKE OF TESCHEN

take the field under the emperor himself, supported by his most famous marshals. A very different spirit animated the Austrians, who had no desire to recommence hostilities, and whose troops discouraged by the memories of their former reverses, entered on the campaign without enthusiasm and with very little hope of eventual success.

Napoleon, who had assumed the title of Emperor in the previous December, had an enormous advantage, in that he had undisputed control of the entire resources, both civil and military, of his empire, while the Allies, besides the difficulties of command inevitable in all coalitions, were hampered by the preposterous Aulic Council which, by directing all military operations from Vienna and interfering with the leaders on the spot, had so often wrecked the combinations of the Austrian generals.

By his decision to advance from the Rhine and the Main, Napoleon gained all the advantages of a rectangular base against the Austrians in the Valley of the Danube, and these were still further accentuated by their suicidal advance to the line of the Iller.

During the first phase of the campaign, the theatre of operations was bounded on the north by the Main, on the south by the mountainous frontiers of Switzerland and the Tyrol, on the West by the Rhine from Basle to Mayence, and on the east by the Bohmer Wald and Inn.

The Danube, rising in the southern portion of the Black Forest, flowed in a north-easterly direction through the theatre of operations as far as Ratisbon, whence it made a bend southward to Passau; on its right bank it was joined by numerous tributaries flowing from the Alps, at right angles across the line of advance into the heart of Austria.

The most important were the Iller, joining the main stream at Ulm, the Loch near Donauwörth, the Isar between Ratisbon and Passau, and the Inn at the latter town. The most formidable obstacle to the French advance into the Valley of the Danube was the Black Forest, a densely wooded, mountainous district extending northward for about a hundred miles from the frontiers of Switzerland, parallel to the Rhine between Basle and

Karlsruhe. It was divided into two unequal parts by the Valley of the Kinzig, a small river flowing into the Rhine at Kehl, opposite Strasburg.

The southern and larger portion was by far the most mountainous and densely wooded, though both were thickly covered by forests of beech, oak and fir. The climate of the Black Forest was wet and inclement, the roads few and bad, quite unfit for the passage of large bodies of troops accompanied by their transport. The breadth of the mountainous tract was about forty miles, and on the west, it fell away sharply towards the Rhine, but its eastern slopes were more gentle, gradually merging into the Suabian Plains. The Rhine, flowing from Lake Constance, and the headwaters of the Danube, approached each other closely north of Schaffhausen, forming a defile through which the direct road *via* Stockach, Memmingen, Landsberg to Munich and Vienna ran.

North of the Danube and parallel to the river, from its source to Donauwörth, were the mountains of the Suabian Jura, continuing after a gap round Nördlingen, through which the Wernitz ran into the Danube, as the Franconian Jura until they reached the Main near Bamberg. From Mannheim, on the Rhine, the Neckar ran first east and then south to Stuttgart round the northern edge of the Black Forest, and to the north again between the latter river and the Main was the mountainous district of the Oden Wald. The Valley of the Neckar was extremely fertile, and though it had suffered severely during the Revolutionary Wars, had, during the recent peace, to a great extent recovered its prosperity.

Between the Danube and the Alps, the Bavarian Plateau was a fertile, well-watered tract of country, chiefly remarkable for its numerous small lakes and marshes, while its inhabitants, like their neighbours in Baden and Wurtemberg, were by no means hostile to the French; in fact, on this occasion, the Bavarians looked on the latter as their deliverers.

Ulm, situated on the borders of Wurtemberg and Bavaria at the junction of the Iller and Danube, was destined to exercise a remarkable influence on the Austrian strategy, probably from the fact that, by holding it, Kray had checked Moreau's advance on

Vienna for a considerable period during the previous campaign.

At any rate, Mack attached enormous importance to its possession, though against an advance from the Main it was little better than a trap and, apart from the fact that it possessed a *tête du pont* on either bank of the Danube and was on the flank of the line of advance from Stockach to Augsburg and Munich, it had few advantages. As a fortress it was of no great importance, for it would have needed a very large garrison to hold the heights surrounding the town, and the large entrenched camp on the Michelsberg to the northward had been allowed to fall into a state of decay; but, for all that, the possession of Ulm exercised a paralyzing effect on Mack's strategy.

In their previous campaigns French troops had, chiefly from the fact that there was no money available to provide transport, lived on the country, but Napoleon had made arrangements for the provision of supplies for the ensuing campaign, though owing to the failure of the contractors to supply wagons, the scheme to a great extent fell through. Consequently the French corps were forced to requisition transport and supplies during their march, and zones were allotted to each commander in which he could forage; but the impressed transport proved of poor quality, and, in spite of the efforts of the French marshals, foraging soon led to pillage and straggling which, by the time the army had crossed the Inn, had grown to an alarming extent.

CHAPTER 2

First Movements

(1) The Austrian Advance into Bavaria—Escape of the Bavarian Army—Disagreement among the Austrian Commanders—Mack's Dangerously Isolated Position.

(2) March of the French Corps to the Rhine and the Main—Demonstration by Murat through the Black Forest—Advance of the French Corps—The Violation of Prussian Territory.

(3) The French Flank March and Wheel to the Right—Expected Battle—Mack's Inactivity.

(1) During the latter part of August, the Austrian Amy destined to act in the Valley of the Danube had assembled at Wels, on the Traun, within three or four marches of the Bavarian frontier. Political as well as military reasons prompted Mack, who, though nominally chief of the staff to the Archduke Ferdinand, was in reality in command of the Austrian force, to counsel an advance into Bavaria. He hoped to force the Elector, whose treaty with Napoleon had remained a secret, to throw in his lot with the Allies and to encourage the rulers of Baden and Wurtemberg to oppose the French advance; also, by removing the theatre of operations from the Austrian Provinces, to spare them the horrors of war. Moreover, he had endeavoured to introduce the French system of living on the country into his army, and his troops, totally unused to this mode of subsistence, were already beginning to feel the pinch of hunger.

The Elector's one aim had been to remain neutral, but on the Austrian emperor's refusal to consent to this course, he had signed a secret treaty with Napoleon, convinced that he had more to fear from the French than from the Austrians. On the

4th of September, Lena, with thirty squadrons and the same number of battalions, advanced in two columns towards the Inn, which formed the Eastern frontier of Bavaria. Four days later the northern column, crossing the river at Schärding, marched *via* Landshut on Freising, with the object of cutting off the retreat of the Bavarian Army, while the southern, crossing at Braunau, occupied Munich on the 11th of September. The Elector meanwhile, retiring first to Ratisbon and eventually to Wurzburg on the Main, ordered his army to concentrate at Bamberg, avoiding, if possible, any collision with the Austrian forces.

The violation of their territory and the proposed breaking up of their army by drafting regiments to the various Austrian corps, aroused the hostility of the inhabitants and threw them into the arms of the French. The Allies' opening move had been singularly unsuccessful, the Bavarian Army had escaped and neither Baden nor Wurtemberg showed the least disposition to oppose the French advance.

From the first the Archduke Ferdinand and Mack had been at variance, the former pointing out that Napoleon, with 150,000 men, could be on the Isar and occupy Munich before the Russians could arrive on the Inn, was in favour of taking up positions to delay the enemy's advance on the Lech and Isar, so as to give the Allies time to complete their concentration. Though he was supported by the Archduke Charles and the other Austrian commanders, he was over-ruled by Mack, who was determined to advance to the Iller and rest his right on Ulm, sending forward the bulk of his mounted troops to watch the eastern exits of the roads through the Black Forest.

It was extremely unfortunate for the Allies that Mack had sufficient influence with the Emperor Francis to carry through his ill-judged scheme in face of the opposition of the Archduke Charles and his brother commanders. Mack, who had an entirely undeserved reputation as a strategist and tactician, had completely imposed on the Emperor of Austria and Pitt; he was industrious and painstaking, over ready with pedantic schemes but devoid of any real ability and quite unable to command the confidence of his subordinates. In the field ho had proved himself an unlucky leader; moreover, he was generally unpopular with the army, which had a very poor opinion of his ability.

Owing to the enormous distance which they had to march, it was clearly impossible for even the First Russian Contingent to arrive in time to take part in the operations on the Iller. Kutusoff had crossed the frontier at Brody with 46,000 men, and was advancing in seven columns, but at the end of August was between two hundred and fifty and three hundred miles from the Inn, and could not possibly concentrate the whole of his force on the eastern frontier of Bavaria much before the 20th of October, while the Second Contingent, under Buxhowden, which had assembled on the Bug and was delayed by the doubtful attitude of Prussia, was not timed to arrive on the Inn until a month later.

Under the existing circumstances, the Archduke Charles' plan of remaining on the defensive behind the Inn until the arrival of the Russians, and assuming a vigorous offensive in Northern Italy, supported by the Archduke John's Army in, the Tyrol, was obviously the correct one. Mack; however, had his way, and crossing the Lech with about 72,000 men on the 15th of September, he advanced to the Iller, occupying Ulm on the 20th. Acting under the entirely erroneous supposition that the French, whose army he believed would not exceed 70,000 men, would follow their traditional line of advance from the middle Rhine through the Black Forest into the Valley of the Danube, he intended to oppose their progress on the Line of the Iller.

His right rested on Ulm at the junction of the Danube and the Iller, his centre was round Memmingen, and his left, stretching beyond Kempten, would enable him to maintain touch with the Tyrol, while on his extreme flank Jellachich would occupy a forward position round Stockach and Lake Constance. Altogether, his force was spread out over a front of about ninety miles, while his want of imagination led him to ignore Napoleon's brilliant stroke at his opponents' communications at the commencement of the Marengo Campaign, and the possibility of a somewhat similar movement round his right flank, which would cut him off from his base and from his Muscovite Allies.

20

BERNHARD ERASMUS VON DEROY
GENERAL OFFICER IN THE BAVARIAN ARMY

(2) When Napoleon definitely made up his mind to abandon his projected invasion of England, on the 24th of August, the different corps of the Grand Army were stationed in cantonments on the shores of the Channel, in Holland, and in Hanover, as follows:—

1st Corps	... Bernadotte	... 17,000 strong	... Hanover
2nd Corps	... Marmont	... 24,000 strong	... Holland
3rd Corps	... Davout	.. 27,000 strong	... Ambleteuse
4th Corps	... Soult	... 40,000 strong	... Boulogne
5th Corps	... Lannes	.. 18,000 strong	... Vimereux
6th Corps	... Ney	... 24,000 strong	... Etaples
7th Corps	... Augereau	... 14,000 strong	... Brittany

The emperor intended to lead these seven corps, together with the Guard, over 7,000 strong under Bessières, and the Cavalry Reserve under Murat, which amounted to some 22,000 men, into the Valley of the Danube, to crush the Austrians ere they could be joined by their Russian Allies, while Massena, with about 50,000 men, was to contain the Archduke Charles in Northern Italy. The right and centre, concentrating on the middle Rhine between Strasburg and Mannheim, were to advance north of the Black Forest, striking the Danube at Donauwörth, while the left wing, consisting of the 1st, 2nd and the Bavarian Corps, 25,000 strong, under the command of Bernadotte, were to advance from the Main to Ingolstadt, lower down the Danube.

Napoleon would thus avoid traversing the difficult tract of country covered by the Black Forest, through which the roads were few and bad, and strike at his opponent's communications with the whole of his formidable force, which, including the Bavarians, numbered well over 200,000 men and 350 guns. To ensure the success of this plan it was necessary that his opponent should remain in ignorance of the true direction of his advance, and be induced to remain on the Iller as long as possible. This vitally important task was allotted to Murat, with the Cavalry Reserve, who, supported by Lannes, was to advance through the Black Forest, and screening the march of the main body, to hold Mack on the Iller by a series of demonstrations.

His force consisted of two divisions of Heavy Cavalry under Nansouty and D'Hautpoul, composed of eight regiments of *cuirassiers* and two regiments of *carabiniers*; three divisions of dragoons of six regiments each, under Klein, Beaumont, and Walther; a division of Light Cavalry of four regiments of hussars and *chasseurs*, under Milhaud; as well as eight battalions of dismounted dragoons, under Bourcier; in all 22,000 men, 14,000 horses, with 14 light and 10 heavier guns. The large proportion of dismounted men was due to the fact that the army had been destined for the invasion of England, and the difficulties presented by transporting a large number of horses across the Channel.

The different corps were so fully prepared to take the field that the emperor's order was all that was needed to set them in motion towards their destined points of concentration on the Rhine and Main. Prince Murat was appointed Lieutenant-General of the Empire on the 30th of August, and charged with the duties of superintending the concentration on the Rhine and the collection of intelligence, until the arrival of the emperor in person.

Five days earlier Murat, travelling *incognito* as "Colonel de Beaumont," made a hasty reconnaissance of the theatre of operations, his route being through Mayence—Wurzburg—Bamberg—Nuremberg—to Ratisbon, thence down the Danube to Passau, up the Inn, across to Munich, and finally *via* Ulm, through the Black Forest to Strasburg, where he arrived in ample time to superintend the concentration of his Cavalry Reserve, about the middle of September.

Savary was also sent to reconnoitre the routes leading from the Rhine, through the Valley of the Neckar, north of the Black Forest, to the Danube, while Bertrand, who was charged with a mission to the Elector of Bavaria, was to obtain as much information as possible about the country.

If the Austrians remained on the defensive on the Inn, which was their obvious course, Napoleon intended to assemble his army in Bavaria before attacking them, but if they advanced towards the Iller he meant to cross the Danube in their rear and interpose between them and their base. In any case he meant

JEAN-BAPTISTE BERNADOTTE, FRENCH MARSHAL,
KING OF SWEDEN, PRINCE DE PONTE CORVO

to strike the Danube between Donauwörth and Ingolstadt, and unite his left with the main body before crossing the river. The march of the Grand Army from the Channel to the Rhine was carried out in the most perfect order; the weather was all that could be desired, and the troops arrived at their destination in splendid condition and full of enthusiasm.

The distance was approximately 300 miles, and Napoleon allowed his corps, on the average, twenty-seven days to complete the journey, which, with an occasional day of rest, made the marches work out at about twelve miles *per diem*. The various stages had been carefully mapped out, and arrangements made in the minutest detail, consequently the corps arrived at their destinations practically without any loss from sickness, straggling or desertion.

Fully aware of the enormous importance of secrecy in military operations, Napoleon used his autocratic powers to the full, muzzling the Press and stopping all letters at the Rhine, so that no rumour of his intentions should reach his opponents.

The movement commenced with the march of Nansouty's Heavy Cavalry to the Rhine on the 26th of August; on the 28th the first divisions of the corps of Davout (3rd), Soult (4th), and Ney (6th) commenced their march, followed on the 30th by the second divisions, and on the 1st of September by the third. Lannes (5th) with two divisions, preceded Ney's corps at a day's interval, one of his divisions (Gazan's) and the fourth division of Soult's Corps followed in the rear of Davout.

The Grand Army made use of three distinct routes in their march from the Channel to the Rhine; the 4th and 6th Corps moved *via* St. Omer—Cambrai—Meziers—Sedan—Verdun to Metz, whence the 4th marched by Landau to Spires, and the 5th through Nancy to Strasburg. The 3rd Corps marched by way of Lille—Namur—Luxemburg—Saarlouis to Mannheim, and the 6th *via* Arras—Laon—Rheims—Vitry—Nancy to Hagonau. The different corps reached the Rhine between the 23rd and 25th of September, while three days later the Guard arrived at Strasburg, where the Headquarters were established.

The 7th Corps (Augereau) which, owing to the long distance it had to traverse, rendering it impossible for it to reach the Rhine until the middle of October, was to form the General Reserve and to protect the right of the Main Army, marched from Brittany *via* Alençon—Lens—Langres—Belfort to Huningen, a few miles north of Basle, and performed some of the stages of its long march in wagons. Marmont (2nd Corps), with two French and one Batavian Division, marched by three roads to Nimeguen and thence to Cologne and Mayence, arriving at the latter town on the 23rd of September, three days before his appointed time. (The Batavian Republic was established in Holland in alliance with France in 1795.)

The bulk of his ammunition and stores had been sent by boat up the Rhine, and, thanks to his excellent arrangements, only nine men fell out during the twenty consecutive days' marching, which at the commencement of a campaign spoke well for the condition of his corps. After a couple of days halt, he proceeded *via* Frankfurt towards Wurzburg, arriving in the vicinity of that town on the 30th of September. Bernadotte, whose corps had been in military occupation of Hanover, left Gottingen on the 12th of September, and passing through Munden, Cassel and Giessen, reached Wurzburg on the 27th. During his march he had been forced to exercise a good deal of diplomacy to avoid complications when passing through Hessian territory, but, thanks to the excellent discipline preserved by his corps, he reached the Main without any *contretemps* with the Hessian authorities.

Before a single man had crossed the Rhine or the Main, the emperor had gained an enormous advantage over his opponent by the strategical deployment of his corps. His main force on the Rhine was opposite his opponent's right, some nine marches from Ulm, while his powerful left wing, on the Main, within six days' march of the Danube, threatened their communications. On the 25th of September, Murat, crossing the Rhine at Kehl, pushed his cavalry through the Black Forest, and slowly driving back the Austrian patrols, convinced Mack that his prediction as to the French line of advance had been correct. As soon as he was clear of the forest, Murat, leaving a screen of cavalry and

GENERAL MARMONT, FRENCH MARSHAL
AND DUKE OF RAGUSA

Bourcier's 8,000 dismounted dragoons to impose upon Mack, moved off to his left to cover the flank of the main advance.

Lannes, who had followed Murat to support him if necessary, now marched *via* Pforzheim to Stuttgart, where he was joined by the emperor, who had left Strasburg with the Guard on the 1st of October. Ney, meanwhile, who had crossed the Rhine at Maxau on the 27th of September, as soon as the road was clear, moved southward towards Stuttgart to take up his position on the extreme right of the line, as his corps was to form the pivot on which the "wheel to the right" was to be made.

On the same date Davout and Soult, crossing at Mannheim and Spires respectively, moved to their right up the Valley of the Neckar. On the 2nd of October the heads of the different columns were on the line Stuttgart—Wurzburg, extending over a frontage of ninety miles, with the Bavarians at Bamberg, some fifty miles further to the left. Murat had handled his cavalry so ably that the advance had been entirely unobserved by the Austrian patrols, and Mack was absolutely in the dark as to his adversary's movements.

Napoleon was acquainted with Mack, of whose abilities he had formed a very low estimate, and was aware that he had occupied Ulm on the 20th of September; he also hoped that Murat's demonstration through the Black Forest would retain him for some time on the Iller.

He never imagined, however, that Mack would remain indefinitely round Ulm, and fully expected to fight a battle on the 6th or 7th of October in the neighbourhood of Nördlingen, on the northern bank of the Danube.

He fully realised the risk of making an oblique march across his opponent's flank to the Danube, and had therefore allotted Murat and Ney the duty of protecting his exposed flank. The objective of the whole army was Donauwörth, in the neighbourhood of which Napoleon intended to cross the Danube, when his right wing would deal with Mack, while his left, occupying Munich, rendered him secure from any interference from the Russians, and his centre, midway between the two, could quickly reinforce either wing should the necessity arise.

31

In spite of the want of supplies—the transport arrangements having almost entirely broken down, owing to the failure of the contractors to provide the requisite number of wagons—and the state of the roads, which rendered the marches extremely arduous, the French corps had pushed forward with remarkable rapidity. To enable the left wing to arrive at its appointed position in time, and to facilitate its junction with the Bavarians, it was necessary for Bernadotte to traverse the isolated Prussian Province of Anspach, which lay in the direct line of advance from the Main to the Danube. The violation of his territory so enraged Frederick William that he almost decided to join the Allies, and Prussia's attitude became extremely menacing.

Mack, meanwhile, had remained inactive, not in the least disturbed by his total ignorance of his opponents' movements; all he had done had been to send Kienmayer with some 12,000 men on the 23rd of September to Ingolstadt, for the purpose of observing the Bavarians and to divert some thirty battalions, originally intended for the archduke's army in Northern Italy, towards the Iller. The bulk of his force, some 55,000 strong, was still between Ulm and Memmingen, while Auffenberg, with 8,000 men from the Tyrol, and Jellachich, with a similar force from the neighbourhood of Lake Constance, were marching to join him.

Giving Mack credit for a certain amount of common sense, Napoleon still anticipated a battle near Nördlingen; writing to Davout on the 3rd of October, he pointed out that the Austrians might cross the Danube at either Ulm, Donauwörth, or Ingolstadt, or possibly at all three points. If they occupied Nördlingen, Davout, with the centre, consisting of his own and Soult's Corps, was to contain them while the other corps acted against their flanks, while if they attacked the left wing (Marmont, Bernadotte and the Bavarians) Davout, followed by Soult, was to march by the shortest road against their flank, and if they moved against the French right from the direction of Ulm, Napoleon, with the Corps of Ney, Lannes and the Guard would be quite strong enough to deal with them.

By the 5th of October the French corps advancing towards

MARSHAL JEAN LANNES, 1ST DUKE OF MONTEBELLO,
PRINCE OF SIEWIERZ

Nördlingen covered a frontage of sixty miles, while on the following day they were on the line Heidenheim—Eichstadt, roughly parallel to the Danube, their front contracted to forty-five miles. In spite of the difficulties of supply and the slate of the roads, Napoleon, urging his corps forward by forced marches, had successfully completed his "wheel to the right" and brought his force to within a day's march of the Danube, in such a position that he could concentrate 100,000 men on either flank during the day.

It was not until the evening of the 4th that Kienmayer's reports of the masses of hostile troops marching on Donauwörth roused Mack from his fatal lethargy; he then decided to take up a fresh position, with his left resting on Ulm and his centre round Günzburg, preparatory to falling on the heads of the French columns as they crossed the Danube.

Accordingly, he ordered Auffenberg to move from Augsburg to Wertingen with eight battalions and thirteen squadrons, to form the advanced guard for his proposed movement; but, learning that Kienmayer had fallen back to Munich and that the enemy were in much greater force and considerably nearer the river than he had supposed, he again changed his mind.

His new plan was to retreat to Augsburg and to hold the line of the Lech, but his men were so exhausted by the continual marches and counter-marches necessitated by his vacillation that they were unable to carry out the movements with the necessary despatch.

CHAPTER 3

Towards Ulm

(1) The Passage of the Danube by the French Corps—
Murat Defeats Auffenberg at Wertingen—Movements of
the French Corps—Ney seizes the Bridge at Günzburg—
Quarrel between Murat and Ney.

(2) Mack's Schemes and Attempt to Break out of Ulm—
Dupont's Action at Haslach—Escape of Werneck's
Force—Ney Captures the Bridge at Elchingen—Mem-
mingen Surrenders to Soult—The Austrians Driven into
Ulm.

(3) Capitulation of Ulm—Murat Pursues the Archduke
Ferdinand and Werneck—Surrender of Werneck—Escape
of the Archduke into Bohemia.

Kienmayer's weak detachments north, of the Danube, principally composed of cavalry under Nostritz, fell back hastily before the advance of the French corps, and, leaving a few small
bodies of troops to destroy the bridges over the river, the Austrian general retired to Munich.

Napoleon ordered his corps to cross the Danube at once
with the exception of Ney, whose strength was brought up to
30,000 by the dismounted dragoons under Baraguey d'Hilliers
and Bourcier, as well as Gazan's Division of Lannes' Corps being placed under his command. He was ordered to remain on
the Brenz, on the northern bank of the Danube, to prevent any
movement against the French communications and check any
attempt to break out northward from Ulm or Günzburg. Murat
and Soult (4th Corps) were to cross at Donauwörth, Cannes (5th
Corps) at Münster, Davout (3rd Corps) and Marmont (2nd) at
Neuburg, Bernadotte (1st) and the Bavarians at Ingolstadt, while

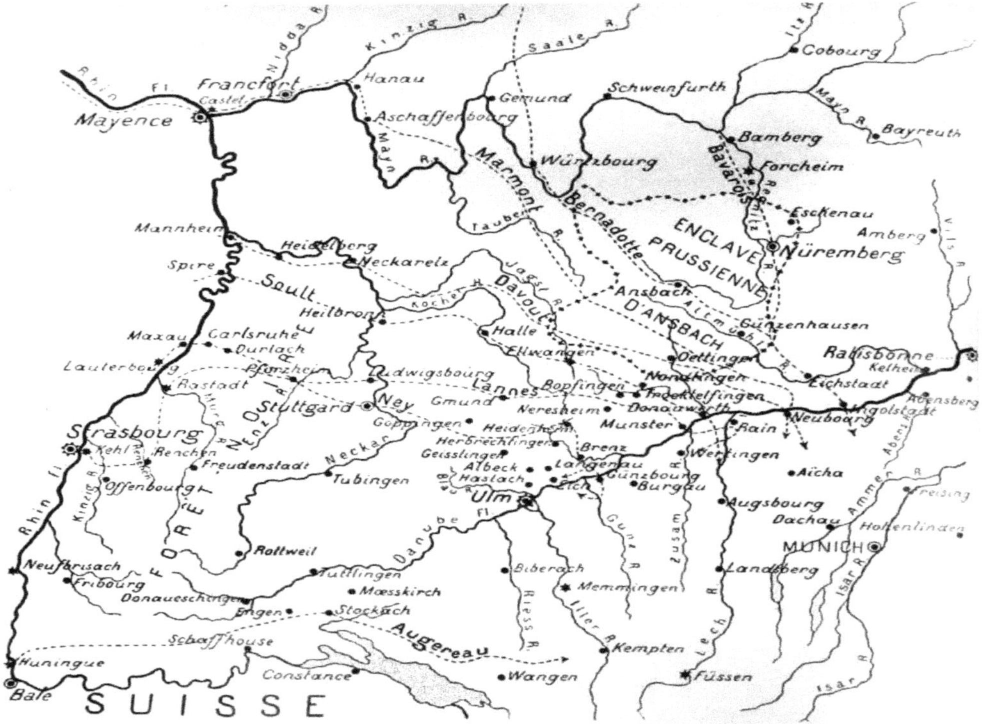

MARCH OF THE GRANDE ARMÉE TO THE DANUBE.

the emperor, with the Guard, was to follow Soult.

On the 7th of October, Murat, finding Soult engaged with the Austrian detachment covering the bridge at Donauwörth, which had been only partially demolished, galloped up the left bank of the river to Münster, where he crossed unopposed. Moving rapidly along the southern bank to the Lech, he chased the Austrian rear-guard from Bain, near the junction of the Danube and Loch, and leaving Walther's Dragoons to hold the line of the latter river, he retraced his steps along the right bank of the Danube, followed by Lannes, who had meanwhile crossed at Münster. Next day his patrols came in contact with the outposts of Auffenberg's detachment, which was halted at Wertingen, on the left bank of the Zusam stream. Auffenberg, who had only arrived there the previous evening, had received orders to fall back to Zusmarshausen to cover the retreat of the main body to Lech, but his men were so exhausted by their purposeless inarches that he had been forced to give them a day of rest.

Taken completely by surprise by the appearance of the French patrols, he sent Dinersberg with a couple of squadrons and four companies towards Pfaffenhoffen to delay the French advance while he made his dispositions for defence. He posted four battalions of grenadiers on the heights in rear of the village on the right of the Günzburg road, a battalion at the Pfaffenhoffen and Augsburg gates, and three battalions in the village itself. Murat, knowing that he was closely followed by Oudinot's grenadiers, decided to attack at once before his opponent could retreat, and his cavalry overthrew Dinersberg's detachment, driving them headlong into the village.

Klein forded the stream with his dragoons above Wertingen, and Exelmans led a couple of regiments of dismounted dragoons across a rickety wooden bridge below the village; the Austrians in Wertingen were now entirely isolated and their cavalry was driven from the field in wild confusion, Auffenberg, throwing the remainder of his infantry into squares, commenced his retreat in tolerable order in spite of the repeated charges of the French cavalry, but his men were soon thrown into hopeless confusion by the deadly fire of Oudinot's grenadiers, who, hastening forward to the sound of the guns, appeared on his left flank and poured in volley after volley with telling effect while the French cavalry renewed their furious assaults.

Square after square broke; the men, flying wildly into the woods, west of Wertingen, lost all cohesion; a large body escaped to Zusmarshausen, afterwards joining Kienmayer, and a further party fled to Günzburg, but the French captured 2,500 prisoners, including the Austrian commander himself, all his baggage and ten guns. Murat's brilliant little victory showed Mack that all hope of retreat to the Lech must be abandoned, and caused him to change his plans once again.

His position was becoming most critical, and though he had made the first move of the campaign, the initiative had soon slipped from his feeble grasp, and he found himself forced to conform to his opponent's movements. Though he could no longer hope to reach the Inn, he could still, provided he acted promptly, make good his escape to the Tyrol, whence he could threaten the flank of the French if they advanced down the Valley of the Danube, and joining the Archduke John, co-operate with the Russians as soon as they arrived on the Inn.

He could also cross the Danube, threaten the French communications, and, marching *via* Nördlingen, regain the river at Passau or retire into Bohemia. But whatever course he chose it behoved him to act with promptitude and vigour, and his army had fallen into such a state of confusion from the continual marches and counter-marches necessitated by his repeated changes of mind, that it was incapable of prompt action.

Napoleon had now completed his great scheme of interposing his whole force between his opponent and his principal base, blocking his direct line of retreat and cutting him off from his Russian allies. He determined to dispose his army in three groups; Murat was given command of the right wing, consisting of the corps of Lannes and Ney, in addition to his own cavalry, and ordered to advance towards Ulm. Bernadotte, with the left wing, composed of his own, Marmont's Corps, and the Bavarians, was to occupy Munich and observe the Russians, while the centre, under the emperor himself, was to occupy a central

CROSSING THE BRIDGE AT ELCHINGEN

position round Augsburg, from which he could reinforce either wing in case of necessity.

To insure communication between the northern and southern banks of the Danube, Ney, who had remained in position round Heidenheim, on the Brenz, was ordered to move southward to Günzburg and seize the bridges over the river near that town, Mack, who had now determined to retreat *via* Nördlingen, had ordered a concentration round Günzburg preparatory to crossing the Danube, and a large portion of his force had arrived near that town, but, as usual, his movements had been much too slow.

Marching at daybreak on the 9th, Ney's Corps reached the river the same evening. His right column experienced some resistance near Albeck, but when Dupont brought up the whole of his division, the enemy retired.

The central column, Loisson's Division, occupied Langeneau and rushed the bridge at Elchingen during the night, meeting with little resistance from the small Austrian detachment stationed there.

On the left, Mahler's Division attacked the bridges round Günzburg in three columns; the central one was unable to force the bridge opposite the town, as the Austrians had a strong force on the far bank and the Archduke Ferdinand hastened up with large reinforcements; on the right, higher up the river, the column destined to seize the crossing at Leipheim lost its way in the marshes and never came into action at all. On the left, however, below Günzburg, the French carried the bridge in great style, in spite of a determined opposition, and the Austrians, abandoning the other two bridges, retired to Ulm during the night with a loss of about 1,500 men, which included over 1,000 prisoners.

Except at Günzburg, where the Archduke himself was present, they had fought in a very half-hearted fashion, and it was evident that, wearied by their purposeless marches and disgusted by Mack's manifest incompetence, they had lost all confidence in their leader.

Ney now found himself under Murat's orders, and was instructed to bring the whole of his corps across to the southern bank of the Danube; to this he demurred, pointing out that with the exceptions of the dismounted dragoons under Baraguey d'Hilliers on the Brenz, and Bourcier's detachment west of Ulm, there were no troops north of the river to protect the communications or to prevent the Austrians retiring towards Bohemia.

A violent quarrel ensued, and though Ney was supported by Lannes, it was only with the greatest difficulty that Murat was persuaded to allow Dupont's division to remain north of the Danube.

Assuming that Mack would adopt the only rational course and retreat as quickly as possible to the Tyrol, Napoleon was most anxious to close his direct route by the capture of Memmingen; he imagined that only a small garrison had been left in Ulm, and that the main Austrian Army was further south, on the right bank of the Iller, in the neighbourhood of Weissenhorn.

Accordingly, the emperor fixed the positions of his corps for the 11th of October as follows—Ney (6th) astride the Danube at Günzburg, Lannes a few miles in rear at Burgau, with Murat's cavalry in front of him on Nay's left. He himself, with Marmont's Corps and the Guard, was at Augsburg, Soult at Landsberg, on his way to Memmingen, Bernadotte and the Bavarians at Munich, with Davout at Dachau, some twelve miles further north.

(2) Urged by the Archduke Ferdinand, Mack, who had concentrated the bulk of his army round Ulm, determined to retreat to Bohemia *via* Nördlingen and Nuremberg. On the 10th of October the Austrians moved across the Danube and bivouacked on the Michelsberg, a range of heights just north of Ulm, except Spangen, who, with 5,000 men, had been ordered to Memmingen.

The men were so exhausted that it was impossible to commence the march until the afternoon of the 11th; Klenau was to move off with the advanced guard at 3 p.m. towards Albeck, on the road to Heidenheim, followed during the evening by the remainder of the army. Werneck, with the rear-guard, was to move off at 3 a.m. on the 12th, and Jellachich, with 6,000 men, was to march up the Iller, breaking down the bridges as he went, and to eventually join Spangen round Memmingen. Had he been able

ENVIRONS
D'ULM.

Une lieue.

to act with promptitude, Murat's blunder in withdrawing the bulk of Ney's Corps to the southern bank of the Danube might have enabled part of the Austrian force to escape, but, as usual, they were too late.

About mid-day on the 11th of October, Dupont, who was on the march towards Ulm, noticed a strong force of the enemy on the heights above Jungingen. He realised at once that the Austrians were in overwhelming strength, and reasoning that if he retired or remained on the defensive, he must inevitably be crushed, he decided to attack. He had marched from Albeck that morning with three infantry and three cavalry regiments and 14 guns, in all about 6,500 men, but he knew that Baraguey d'Hilliers, who had passed the night at Langenau, a few miles in rear, had received orders to support him, and he hoped that if he pressed his attack boldly the Austrians would imagine his little force to be the advance guard of Ney's corps.

He posted the 9th Infantry across the road from him in front of the village of Haslach, the 32nd were on their left and the 96th in reserve, and the 1st Hussars covering the left flank. The Austrians, deceived by the resolute bearing of their opponents, imagined them to be the advance guard of Ney's Corps, and wasted some time in deploying their troops on the heights; eventually they launched a strong column of infantry, covered by their powerful artillery, and preceded by numerous squadrons, against the French right; at the same time other smaller columns descended from the heights against the centre.

The enemy's strong attack on his right flank forced Dupont to bring up the 96th on the outer flank of the 9th, while a battalion of the 32nd were placed in a wood slightly in advance of the main line to further strengthen the threatened flank.

Without waiting to be attacked, the 9th and 96th dashed at their opponents with the bayonet, throwing them into hopeless confusion and taking nearly 2,000 prisoners; the fight then raged fiercely round the village of Jungingen, which was taken and retaken several times. Though the French cavalry charged bravely, they were overwhelmed by the Austrian squadrons, who, sweeping round the flanks, captured the whole of the baggage, including Ney's military chest.

The French guns were almost entirely silenced by the powerful Austrian artillery, but their infantry gallantly held their own against more than fourfold odds, continually charging vigorously into the ranks of their opponents. Eventually, after night had fallen, Dupont retreated to Albeck, leaving over six hundred of his heroic division on the field, but carrying with him 4,000 prisoners and having inflicted a loss of nearly 2,000 killed and wounded on his assailants. His splendid stand rendered the attempt of the Austrians to break out towards Bohemia abortive, and Mack had been so impressed by his determined resistance that he ordered his wearied troops to counter-march to Ulm.

Disheartened by their leader's feeble strategy and disgusted by their purposeless exertions, they had fought with very little spirit, and it was obvious that their morale had deteriorated to an alarming extent. The credit of this most important success was entirely due to Dupont and his gallant division, for Baraguey d'Hilliers, though close at hand, had made no move to support him.

Seeing that Murat was obviously unable to conduct the operations, Napoleon hastened to the spot and most unjustly blamed Ney for unnecessary exposing an isolated division; he ordered Marmont to close towards the Danube, bridges to be thrown across the river, and Ney to retake the bridge at Elchingen, which had been abandoned on Dupont's retreat.

The archduke insisted on another attempt being made to escape northward, and Mack reluctantly gave the necessary orders; Schwarzenberg was to remain at Ulm and make a demonstration southward, while Werneck, with the reserve artillery and baggage, was to march towards Heidenheim; Riesch meanwhile was to take up a position on the Heights of Elchingen to cover the flank of the march and then follow the main body. The movement commenced on the 13th of October, but, delayed by bad roads and encumbered by the enormous train, Werneck only managed to cover about fifteen miles, and Riesch remained on the heights overlooking Elchingen.

On the morning of the 14th Ney advanced with Loisson's

BATTLE OF ELCHINGEN, 14TH OCTOBER, 1805

Division, roughly 7,000 strong, 2,000 cavalry and 11 guns, to force the crossing at the bridge of Elchingen, which had been partially destroyed.

He found the Austrians drawn up on the heights on the opposite bank of the river; their right rested on Thalfingen, whence the ground fell abruptly to the Danube, their centre was on the high ground behind Elchingen, the Abbey and village were strongly held and the left extended to Unter Elchingen, while their artillery was in position on the heights covering the river. Ney launched Villatte's Brigade, composed of the 6th and 39th Regiments, against the bridge, the roadway of which had been torn up; and, covered by the guns, the light companies, crossing by the girders, spread out as skirmishers while the pioneers repaired the bridge.

The remainder of the brigade then crossed, and deploying, advanced against the village. Though they pressed their attack gallantly they were met by a dogged resistance; the second brigade crossed to support them, but it was not until Mahler's Division, which had crossed the river lower down, approached Unter Elchingen, that the strongly built abbey, which was the key of the position, was taken after a desperate resistance.

Riesch now formed his men into squares to resist Ney's furious attacks, but, seeing his left flank menaced, he commenced to retreat, though two of his regiments, throwing themselves into a wood, held out for a considerable time with the most undaunted gallantry, in spite of their heavy losses. Ney, who had been stung by Murat's taunts, gained a most brilliant victory, for which he was most fittingly rewarded with the title of the Duke of Elchingen. During the battle he had exposed himself most recklessly, and his presence in the thick of the fight, dressed in full uniform with all his decorations, had roused his men to a pitch of the greatest enthusiasm.

Once again the unfortunate Mack's attempt to retreat had been frustrated; in fact, the fatal 14th of October finally sealed his fate, for on the same day as his main body fell back under the walls of Ulm, Memmingen had surrendered to Soult, thus finally closing his direct road to the Tyrol.

Next day, Ney made a flank march towards the Michelsberg, north of Ulm. He was replaced at Elchingen by Lannes, while Klein's dragoons, Nansouty's *cuirassiers*, and the Imperial Guard crossed to the northern bank, and Marmont's corps moved up the river.

On the same evening, after a violent quarrel with Mack, the Archduke Ferdinand, determined not to be caught in the trap, left Ulm, with twelve squadrons, to join Werneck. Next day the circle of investment was completed, for Murat's cavalry, galloping through Haslach, joined hands with one of Soult's Divisions which had pushed forward to Laupheim, on the Biberach road, south-west of Ulm. On the 15th the French Corps closed in on the doomed town; Bourcier's detachment were on the extreme right, west of Ulm; then came Ney, opposite the Michelsberg, with Lannes on his left near Haslach; Headquarters and the Guard were at Elchingen; south of the Danube, Marmont advanced towards the town in the angle formed by the latter river and the Iller, while Soult closed in on his left.

During the day Ney drove the Austrians from the Michelsberg, while Suchet, on his left, was equally successful, occupying the suburbs and seizing one of the gates of the town itself. The French batteries on the heights north of Ulm completely dominated the town, which was crowded with the dispirited and disorganised Austrian infantry, and there was nothing to prevent the emperor carrying the place by assault; but having attained his object, he preferred not to risk the losses which would have been entailed by storming the fortifications. Next day, the 16th, he sent a flag of truce to Mack, pointing out to him his hopeless position and demanding his surrender, and on the latter refusing his demand, recommenced the bombardment of the town.

During the day the rain came down in torrents, and a violent hurricane destroyed the bridges below Ulm, temporarily severing all communication between the northern and southern banks of the Danube, but the Austrians were much too disorganised to take advantage of the occurrence.

(3) At first. Mack had loudly announced his intention of holding out to the last, but his courage failed him when Na-

CAPITULATION OF ULM

poleon threatened to take the town by storm, and after some fruitless endeavours to obtain better terms, he agreed to surrender on the 25th, unless he was relieved before that date. The Austrian leader had now entirely lost his nerve, (and, terrified by Napoleon's threats, he signed the capitulation on the 19th, and next day marched out of Ulm, laying down his arms and surrendering 30,000 men, 3,000 horses and 60 guns.

Werneck, meanwhile, had remained near Heidenheim on the 14th, in order to allow his convoy to get well on its way; he had heard the sound of the guns at Elchingen, but, in doubt as to the result of the battle, could not make up his mind to any decided course of action. Next day, sending a strong escort with his convoy, he returned with the bulk of his force towards Ulm, but, before he had made much progress, he came in contact with part of Dupont's Division, near Albeck.

Hesitating what course to pursue, he was still further bewildered by receiving an order from Mack to return to Ulm, and instructions from the archduke to join him at Aalen; as it was obviously impossible to comply with the former, he turned about and retraced his steps towards Heidenheim.

At first Napoleon had been entirely unaware that any large body of the Austrians had escaped, and imagined that the troops engaged with Dupont were only fugitives from Riesch's Corps; however, as soon as he was aware of the true state of affairs, he ordered Murat to take up the pursuit.

Marching on the 16th, the latter overtook the Austrian rearguard between Albeck and Heidenheim; overthrowing them, he pressed forward, and severely harassed the main body, capturing a number of prisoners.

Next morning, when Werneck, after a fatiguing night march, was approaching Aalen, he received an order to branch off through Neresheim to Nördlingen; halting at the former town, he was again overtaken by the French cavalry and forced to continue his march, though a large body of his unfortunate infantry, too exhausted to move, surrendered without offering the slightest resistance.

Marching all night, he halted a few miles short of Nördlingen on the morning of the 18th, sending his cavalry forward to join the archduke at Oettingen.

Almost immediately the French cavalry again appeared, and Werneck's wretched men, who had been reduced to under 2,000 and were physically incapable of further exertions, laid down their arms without resistance.

Remorselessly continuing the pursuit, Murat pressed on towards Nuremberg, capturing hundreds of stragglers as well as the whole of the Austrian reserve artillery and train, but the archduke, with about 2,000 horsemen, managed with great difficulty to escape across the Bohemian frontier, after a running fight lasting two days.

Murat halted at Nuremberg on the 20th of October, having covered over a hundred miles in five days, besides having fought several skirmishes, captured about 15,000 men, 128 guns, and over a thousand wagons.

He received a well-earned meed of praise for his vigorously conducted pursuit, which had completed the destruction of Mack's force, but, remarkable as his rate of progress had been, the extraordinary marching of Oudinot's grenadiers, who had been sent to support him, was even more remarkable.

The first phase of the campaign, had come to a most triumphant conclusion; in less than a month after his corps had crossed the Rhine, Napoleon had driven the Austrians from Bavaria, annihilated Mack's army, thrown the Allies on the defensive, and entirely disorganised all their plans.

Their faulty strategy had given him an opportunity of which he had taken the fullest advantage, while their premature assumption of the offensive had ended in the most complete fiasco and had proved fatal to their chances of ultimate success. Entirely without confidence in their leader, the Austrian troops had fought in a most half-hearted manner, nearly 60,000 of them having surrendered since the commencement of the campaign.

It is difficult to say to what extent Mack was responsible for these disasters, and to what extent they were due to the interference of the Aulic Council, which, by insisting on directing the operations from Vienna, had invariably prevented the success of

GENERAL MACK AT THE CAPITULATION OF THE AUSTRIAN ARMY, ULM, 1805

the Austrian Armies.

But it is certain that under a more resolute leader the troops would have fought with their habitual courage, and that it was entirely due to his weakness and to his continually changing his plans that their morale deteriorated to such a remarkable extent.

One of the most extraordinary features of the campaign is that Mack should have been so entirely in the dark with regard to Napoleon's great turning movement round his right flank, though, of course, the emperor took all possible precautions to deceive his opponent, and Murat handled his cavalry with the most consummate skill.

Still, the fact remains that with a force of 70 squadrons much might have been done, but, apparently, the Austrian leader had very little idea of the proper role of mounted troops, and had taken no precautions to obtain early information of his opponent's movements.

On the whole, probably the fairest verdict is that the faulty strategy of the Allies was primarily responsible for the unfavourable position in which the army found itself, but that Mack's gross incompetence and want of energy was the cause of the magnitude of the disaster.

Possibly the fact that he had so strongly insisted on the importance of Ulm, and was unwilling to stultify himself by abandoning it, was in part responsible for his half-hearted attempts to retreat, but even a few days before he was compelled to surrender, he believed a rumour that a British force had landed in northern France, causing a revolution in Paris, which would force Napoleon to retreat.

The weather, which up to the time the French troops crossed the Danube had been, on the whole, favourable, had since broken, becoming intensely cold and wet. Though this was responsible for a great amount of suffering and misery among the French troops, their opponents suffered even more, and were completely exhausted by their continual marches and countermarches occasioned by Mack's perpetual changes of plan.

CHAPTER 4

The Russians Pursued

(1) Napoleon's Plans—The French Concentration round Munich—Kutusoff Determines to Fall Back—His Preparations for Retreat.

(2) The French Advance—Passage of the Inn—Rearguard Actions—The Fight at Amstetten—Reorganisation of the French Army at Linz.

(3) Kutusoff Crosses the Danube—Defeat of Mortier at Dürrenstein—The French Occupy Vienna—Murat Seizes the Florisdörf Bridge.

(4) Pursuit of the Russians—Bagration's Action at Hollabrünn—Junction of the Allies—Napoleon Occupies Brünn.

(1) Though the capture and destruction of Mack's isolated force had brought the first phase of the campaign to a triumphant conclusion, Napoleon's situation was becoming daily more critical. Prussia's attitude was becoming increasingly hostile, and it was evident that within a few weeks he might have to deal with her army, 150.000 strong, operating from the line of the Main against his communications, which would become increasingly vulnerable as he advanced down the valley of the Danube. If the Allies could concentrate their forces, he would also have to deal with the united Russo-Austrian Army, nearly 200,000 strong.

Under these circumstances, the ordinary commander might well have hesitated, or even fallen back towards the Rhine, in order to shorten his communications, but Napoleon at once determined on the bolder course.

He decided to strike at his nearest opponent, Kutusoff, crush

Austrian General Karl Philipp, Fürst zu Schwarzenberg

him, and then, pushing forward rapidly, to defeat the main body of the Allies before they could be joined by the Archduke Charles's troops from Italy, or Prussia could make up her mind to a decisive course of action.

Time was again the all-important factor in the proposed operations, but, before advancing, it was necessary to organise large supply depots on the line of communications at Ulm, Augsburg, and on the Lech, allot garrisons for their defence; and concentrate the various corps round Munich.

The emperor intended to advance in three columns; Lannes was to move on the left; Murat, with his cavalry, formed the advanced guard for the centre, which was composed of the corps of Soult, Davout, and the Guard; while Bernadotte, Marmont, and the Bavarians, moving on a broad front, would form the right wing of the army. Under the terms of the capitulation, Ney's Corps was to remain round Ulm until the 25th, consequently he was charged with the care of the prisoners.

His corps was practically broken up, for Loisson's Division, with the bulk of the cavalry, was to remain at Ulm to guard the prisoners, Dupont was to follow the main body, while the Marshal himself, with the reminder of his corps, was to subdue the Tyrol and cover the right flank of the advance of the main army on Vienna.

Augereau, who had crossed the Rhine at Huningen, a few miles north of Basle, towards the end of October, and was advancing between the head waters of the Danube and Lake Constance, was to co-operate in the operations in the Tyrol, as well as to furnish garrisons for Augsburg and depots on the line of communications. Meanwhile the several columns of Kutusoff's Russian contingent had arrived on the Inn between the 11th and 20th of October.

As soon as it had been known that Napoleon, with his main army, was advancing from the Rhine, Kutusoff had been urged to hasten his march, and wagons had been supplied by the Austrians in which his men had covered some stages of their long journey; in spite of this, however, the forced marches over the execrable roads had proved so arduous that he had left behind over 6,000 sick and stragglers, while his men arrived on the Inn utterly exhausted. He was entirely unaware of Mack's movements, as his cavalry patrols could obtain no information, and were constantly captured by the enemy.

Kienmayer, with some 18,000 men, who had been cut off from their army when the French crossed the Danube at Ingolstadt, as well as some detachments of Austrian cavalry, joined him, but it was not until Mack himself arrived on the 23rd of October on his way to Vienna, that the Russian commander learned of the Capitulation of Ulm. With barely 50,000 men, it was obviously impossible for him to maintain his forward position on the Inn, so he wisely determined to fall back slowly to join the second contingent, under Buxhowden, delaying his opponent as much as possible to gain time for the Archduke Charles to effect his junction with the Army of the Allies.

Sending off his sick, baggage, stores and reserve ammunition at once, he concentrated his main body round Braunau, ordered an Austrian detachment to Passau, on the Danube, to cover his right, while Kienmayer moved to Salzburg, on the Salsbach, a tributary of the Inn, to protect his left. Prince Bagration was to command the rear-guard, which Miloradovitch, with a strong reserve, was to precede by a half-day's march. Leaving a few weak detachments on the Inn to delay the enemy's crossing, Kutusoff evacuated Braunau on the 26th of October, marching by Altheim and Ried towards the Traun, which he intended to cross at Weis and Lambach.

(2) Commencing his advance, the same day, Napoleon, whose object was, if possible, to surround the Russians, ordered his right to push rapidly forward across the head waters of the various streams flowing from the Tyrol into the Danube. If his opponent attempted to defend the lower reaches of the rivers, the emperor intended to turn their flank with his right, while Lannes interposed between them and the Danube. The destruction of the bridges had little effect in delaying the French advance; Bernadotte drove off the small hostile detachment, crossing at Wasserberg and Rosenheim, where Marmont also crossed, and entered Salzburg unopposed.

General Karl Freiherr Mack

Lower down the Inn, Davout forced a passage at Mühldorf, whereupon Murat, crossing with his cavalry, scattered a small hostile detachment which had been left to observe the river. Lannes, finding the enemy had evacuated Braunau, ferried his corps across in boats provided by the inhabitants, and found in the town large supplies of food and ammunition, as well as several guns which, owing to want of transport, the Russians had been forced to abandon. As Braunau, as well as being situated at an important crossing, was strongly fortified, Napoleon decided on making it a secondary base, ordering up large supplies of stores and provisions which had been accumulated at Augsburg.

During the 29th and 30th of October the whole French Army had successfully crossed the Inn, and on the latter day Murat, pushing forward with his cavalry, drove back a rear-guard which had taken up a position near Ried. On the 31st he again overtook them, but found them supported by eight battalions of Russian infantry covering the demolition of the bridge over the Traun at Lambach, who were only driven back, after an obstinate struggle, by a division of Davout's corps when the destruction had been successfully accomplished.

On the 1st of November, Napoleon determined to concentrate on the Traun before continuing his advance through the narrow tract of country between the Danube and the northern spurs of the Tyrolean Alps. Lannes was ordered to Linz, at the junction of the Traun and Danube; Davout assembled his corps at Lambach; Soult occupied Wels, while Bernadotte closed to the left, towards the body, sending the Bavarians under Deroi towards the Tyrol, to co-operate with Ney.

With the exception of Bagration's rear-guard, the Allies had crossed the Enns; their main body halted at the town of Enns, and Merveldt's Austrians higher up the river at Steyer. The Emperor of Austria ordered Kutusoff to hold the line of the river as long as possible, then to fall back to the bridge head in process of construction at Mautern, on the Danube, opposite Krems. The Russian commander, however, had no intention of risking his army for the purpose of covering Vienna, and, learning that Merveldt had been defeated by Davout, at Steyer, on the 4th of

November, he fell back to Amstetten. On the 5th of November Murat encountered Bagration, who, with thirteen battalions and some squadrons, had taken up a position across the road in a clearing in the forest near Amstetten, to check the pursuit, which had become inconveniently close.

Murat at once attacked impetuously with his cavalry, but met with no success, though he was supported by Oudinot's grenadiers; Miloradovitch brought up some fresh battalions from, the reserve, and the struggle continued with renewed fury. Murat's attempts to turn the Russian flanks failed, whereupon Miloradovitch launched a vigorous counter-stroke against the French centre, driving back Oudinot's grenadiers at the point of the bayonet. Throughout the day, in spite of the bitter cold and the heavy fall of snow, the battle raged desperately, neither side gaining much advantage; but eventually, long after darkness had fallen, the Russians were forced to retire, pursued by Murat's hussars, who captured over a thousand prisoners.

Napoleon, meanwhile, had established his headquarters at Linz, where he remained until the 9th of November. He determined to form a new corps, to co-operate north of the Danube with the main advance, threaten the Allies' communications with Moravia, and, if possible, seize the bridge at Krems, the only means of crossing the river between Linz and Vienna.

The force was composed of Klein's dragoons, a division of the corps of Ney (Dupont's), Lannes (Gazan's), and Marmont (Dumonceau's), under the command of Mortier, who was instructed to move north of the Danube, keeping slightly in rear of Lannes, who was advancing on the southern bank of the river, and to maintain communication with him by means of a flotilla of boats, which had been formed under the command of a naval officer.

On the 7th of November Murat occupied the famous Abbey of Mölk, narrowly missing capturing the Emperor of Austria, who only quitted the building a short time before the arrival of the French cavalry, while next day Davout again attacked Merveldt, completely defeating him at Mariazell, at the foot of the Tyrolean Mountains. On the same day, the 8th of November.

General Davout, 1st Duke of Auerstaedt, 1st Prince of Eckmühl, French Marshal

Kutusoff had taken up his position on the edge of St. Pölten, the last spot suitable for defence before reaching Vienna, and Napoleon, hoping that at last he had brought his wily antagonist to action, made elaborate preparations to envelop his flanks.

But the Russian commander was much too able a general to risk the annihilation of his army for the sake of protecting the Austrian capital, and, skilfully slipping away, he crossed the Danube at Krems, burning the long wooden bridge behind him, and leaving only a screen formed by Kienmayer's weak corps to hold the position. Murat, unable to resist the temptation of capturing Vienna, drove the small Austrian force before him and, closely followed by Lannes, established himself within a few miles of the Austrian capital on the 11th of November.

He immediately sent patrols along the banks of the river to collect boats, as well as towards Hungary and Styria, but, during the evening, he received a peremptory order to halt from the emperor, who was furious at the escape of the Russians, who, by burning the bridge, had temporarily checked all pursuit and were in a position to crush Mortier's isolated corps.

Murat had pushed forward along the excellent main road south of the Danube so rapidly that Mortier, delayed by the bad road and difficult country north of the river, had been hardly to keep pace in spite of the long marches he had made; his divisions were nearly a day's march apart, and his cavalry, which should have been thrown well forward, was a considerable distance away on his left flank, reconnoitring towards Bohemia. Once safely across the Danube, with the bridge at Krems burnt behind them, the Russians, free from immediate pursuit, had three courses open to them:

(1) They could continue their retreat to join Buxhowden in Moravia;

(2) march along the northern bank of the Danube to oppose the French attempts to cross at Vienna;

(3) fall on Mortier's isolated corps, defeat it and remain in position near Krems threatening the hostile communications or retire slowly to effect their junction with the

main body.

Kutusoff decided to crush Mortier and remain in position at Krems until the arrival of Buxhowden, where he would be perfectly safe as long as the Austrians held the bridge at Florisdörf, over the main arm of the Danube, east of Vienna. The road by which the French were advancing ran through a narrow defile, formed by the rooky heights which bordered the bend of the Danube between the villages of Weissenkirchen and Dürrenstein; the country between the latter village (which was situated at the eastern exit of the defile) and Stein, on the western outskirts of Krems, was more open, passing through fields and vineyards intersected by low stone walls.

On the heights north of Dürrenstein was the castle in which Richard I. of England had been confined on his return from the Holy Land, and between the village and Stein were situated the two small hamlets of Ober and Unter Loiben. Kutusoff's plan, which had been suggested to him by the Austrian General Schmidt, was to hold the French in front with a small force, while a strong column, making a detour northward through the mountains, fell in overwhelming strength on their flank and seized the defile in their rear. He was well aware that the French divisions were a considerable distance apart, and did his best, by means of spies and pretended deserters, to lead his opponent to believe that only a weak rear-guard remained in Krems.

He posted Miloradovitch, with six battalions, on the outskirts of Stein, while Dochtoroff, with twenty-one battalions, marched through the mountains to fall on the French flank, and the remainder of his force formed the reserve to support Miloradovitch, if necessary. On the night of the 10th of November, Mortier, who was with Gazan's Division, which was leading the advance, bivouacked at Dürrenstein and Ober Loiben, Dupont at Spitz, some distance in rear of the defile, while Dumonceau was still farther to the rear.

Convinced that he had only a weak rear-guard to deal with, the French marshal determined to attack at once, without waiting for his other two divisions, as he was afraid that the Russians might escape him. He advanced on the morning of the 11th,

GENERAL NICOLAS CHARLES OUDINOT,
1ST DUKE OF REGGIO, FRENCH MARSHAL

about 8 a.m., but almost immediately encountered Miloradovitch, who had moved forward to meet him.

At first, after a furious struggle round Unter Loiben, Gazan's
infantry made some progress, but, supported by some battalions
from the reserve, the Russians again returned to the attack, capturing a battery which had been playing on their dense columns
with great effect. The guns were taken and retaken several times,
but in spite of their utmost efforts the French could gain little
ground, and when a fresh regiment made a fierce attack on his
left flank from the direction of Egelsee, Mortier at last realised
that he was engaged with Kutusoff's main body, not a weak
rear-guard as he had imagined. He determined to fall back on
Dürrenstein, at the eastern exit of the defile, and hold the village
until Dupont's Division could arrive to reinforce him.

During the afternoon there was a lull in the combat, and
Mortier, leaving a rear-guard to check Miloradovitch, commenced his retreat to Dürrenstein. Kutusoff, meanwhile, had
been anxiously awaiting the arrival, on the heights overlooking
the defile, of Dochtoroff's columns, which had been timed to
fall on the French early in the morning; but, misled by their
guides and delayed by the difficulties of the road, the left column
only appeared at Dürrenstein late in the afternoon, while the
other columns debouched from the mountains even later.

The small French garrison was driven out of the village, and
Mortier found himself between two fires, for as soon as he had
commenced his retreat, Miloradovitch had again advanced. Both
sides fought with the most desperate valour, Mortier himself being especially conspicuous for his cool courage, but the French,
crowded together, suffered heavily from the Russian fire. Darkness had fallen, but the fight still raged fiercely in the pelting
rain, for Dupont, marching to the sound of the guns, was hotly
engaged with the second Russian column round Weissenkirch-
en, at the western entrance of the defile.

Leaving a portion of his force to engage the third column,
which was about to debouch from the mountains, Dupont's
men steadily forced their way forward, plying butt and bayonet
furiously in a series of hand-to-hand combats. Dochtoroff was

now caught between the two French divisions and, after a desperate struggle, Dupont's men, cheering lustily, forced their way at the point of the bayonet into the village from the west at the same moment as the remnant of Gazan's sorely-tried division entered from the opposite side.

Dochtoroff was now compelled to retire, his men falling back sullenly, but in excellent order, while Mortier's two divisions were so exhausted by their twelve hours' continuous marching and fighting, that the marshal retreated to Spitz, where he found the flotilla of boats and transported his men to the southern bank of the Danube during the night.

Thanks to their splendid gallantry, Gazan's Division had escaped annihilation, while Dupont, by his determined advance to extricate his commander, had given a fresh proof of his courage and ability, but the true reason of the failure of Kutusoff's able scheme was the unforeseen delay which prevented Dochtoroff's columns coming into action at the appointed time. Both sides lost heavily in the fiercely contested battle, the Russian casualties amounting to about 2,000 men, while the French, including prisoners, lost rather more, as well as five guns.

During the day Napoleon, who could obtain no definite information as to the progress of the action, had been a prey to the most intense anxiety, and he was profoundly relieved when he learned that Mortier's Corps had escaped destruction.

Next day, the 12th of November, Murat was ordered to occupy Vienna and at all costs gain possession of the Florisdörf bridge, while Bernadotte was instructed to throw a bridge over the Danube at either Mölk or Krems and continue the pursuit of the Russians.

On the morning of the 13th, Murat and Lannes, approaching the long bridge over the main arm of the Danube east of Vienna, found it prepared for demolition and covered by batteries supported by infantry drawn up on the far bank. As it was obviously impossible to take it by force, Murat had recourse to a ruse: sending a staff officer with a flag of truce to the Austrian commander, he informed him that an armistice had been concluded, and accompanied by Lannes and a few of his staff, crossed the

MARSHAL GENERAL JEAN-DE-DIEU SOULT,
1ST DUKE OF DALMATIA

bridge to speak to Count Auersperg.

Meanwhile, Oudinot's grenadiers, who had unostentatiously approached, suddenly charged across the bridge at the double, while an engineer officer cut the powder hose unnoticed in the confusion. Taken entirely by surprise, the artillery commander was seized by the throat by Murat before he could give the order to fire, and the crossing was gained without the loss of a single man. The unscrupulous trick was brilliantly successful, the Austrian commander, Count Auersperg, withdrew his troops without attempting any resistance, and the possession of the bridge rendered Kutusoff's position at Krems untenable.

As a matter of fact, the Russian commander, who was well served by his spies, heard of the capture of the bridge the same evening, and during the night commenced his retreat, leaving his wounded behind him at Krems. His position was extremely critical, as to effect his junction with Buxhowden, who was hurrying forward by forced marches to join him, he would have to move *via* Zniam to Brünn, exposing his right flank to attack from Vienna.

Napoleon lost no time in taking up the pursuit; Murat, supported by Soult and Lannes, moved northward, *via* Stockerau, to intercept the Russians before they could pass Zniam, where the roads from Vienna and Krems to Brünn joined, and Bernadotte, supported by Mortier, followed them up from Krems.

On the afternoon of the 15th of November the French cavalry came in contact with the Russian flank guard under Bagration, who had taken up a strong position round Hollabrünn to cover the march of the main body. Anxious to hold them until his infantry arrived, Murat entered into negotiations with Bagration, but the latter referred him to Kutusoff, who was close at hand with the main body.

The wily Russian, who was only too anxious to gain time, completely deceived Murat by sending Prince Winzingerode, A.D.C. to the Russian Emperor, to propose an armistice. Murat agreed, halting his troops and referring the matter to the emperor, while Kutusoff pushed rapidly forward to Zniam, under cover of the flank guard, which Bagration had meanwhile withdrawn to Schoengraben, a few miles north of Hollabrünn. (Schoengraben, Grund and Guntersdorf are three small villages a short distance apart on the road to Zniam, north of Hollabrünn.)

Napoleon at once saw through the ruse, and, furious with Murat, who had let the Russians slip through his hands, he ordered him to attack at once.

Bagration had again retreated a short distance, taking up his position in front of the village of Grund, which had been prepared for defence. Late on the afternoon of the 16th of November Murat, who, besides his cavalry, had with him Oudinot's grenadiers and Suchet's division of Lannes's corps, as well as Vandamme's and Legrand's divisions of Soult's corps, launched his attack. Bagration had posted his guns in front of Grund, sweeping the road from Hollabrünn, on either side of which the bulk of his infantry was drawn up; his squadrons protected his flanks, and he also held the village itself.

Oudinot advanced against the hostile centre along the main road, with Legrand on his left and Suchet on his right, while Vandamme's division remained some distance in rear on the road from Hollabrünn, in reserve, and the cavalry, pushing forward, tried to cut off the enemy's retreat by working round his flanks. Oudinot's Grenadiers, delayed for some time by the blazing village of Schoengraben, which had been set on fire by the Russian guns, eventually forced the hostile infantry to fall back into the village of Grund. On the extreme left, however, the French cavalry were repulsed and the Russian infantry retired slowly, in perfect order; but on the other flank Lannes had attacked in force, and it was only by sheer hard fighting that the enemy's two regiments made good their retreat.

In Grund itself the fight raged furiously, but Bagration, handling his men with rare ability, managed to retire in tolerable order to Güntersdorf, where he had previously posted a couple of battalions and a few Cossacks.

Here the Russians offered a desperate resistance, and after a confused struggle, lasting till midnight, Bagration managed to cut his way through his opponents with his gallant rear-guard, now reduced to a little over 3,000 men. With only 7,000 men against Murat's 25,000, the Russian general had conducted the action with great ability, and thanks to his own skill and the dogged courage of his men, he had saved the main body, enabling them to get clear away. Two days later he rejoined Kutusoff, who had effected his junction with Buxhowden and Liechtenstein at Wischau, between Olmütz and Brünn, on the 18th of November.

The Allies continued their retreat, eventually going into cantonments round Olschan, some five miles south-west of Olmütz. Their united forces now amounted to about 80,000 men; Kutusoff had brought in 35,000, Buxhowden 27,000, and Liechtenstein some 16,000. Murat, followed by the main body, entered Brünn unopposed on the 19th of November, and two days later his cavalry defeated the Allied squadrons in a brilliant action at Rausnitz, on the road to Olmütz.

Napoleon himself arrived at Brünn on the 20th, and fixed his headquarters in the town, while Murat, after his successful skirmish, remained at Rausnitz, throwing a screen of horsemen well forward to maintain touch with the enemy.

With the French occupation of Brünn, the second phase of the campaign came to a close, and though it had not proved so conclusively successful as the operations which culminated in the capitulation of Ulm and the destruction of Mack's army, much had been accomplished.

Though Napoleon had failed in his main object, the destruction of Kutusoff's Russian contingent, principally owing to Murat's blundering during the advance to Vienna and in the action against Bagration near Hollabrünn, the Russian general had certainly stolen a march on him by the able manner in which he had slipped away from the St. Polten position and temporarily checked all pursuit by burning the bridge at Krems.

As it happened, Mortier's reverse at Dürrenstein was counterbalanced by the successful but unscrupulous ruse by which Murat gained possession of the Florisdörf Bridge, but, all the same, Napoleon was greatly mortified by Kutusoff's hardly-won victory.

However, the rapid occupation of a large part of! the Austrian Empire, and the moral and material gain derived from possession of Vienna, was a distinct triumph for the French arms.

To have freed Bavaria, destroyed one hostile army, over-run Northern Italy and the Tyrol, occupied Vienna and chased the Allied Armies into a corner of the Austrian Dominions was no mean feat, even for Napoleon and the Grand Army, especially as it had all been accomplished in less than two months from the date on which the French Corps had crossed the Rhine.

CHAPTER 5

Prelude to Austerlitz

(1) Napoleon Halts at Brünn—Distribution of the French Corps—Napoleon Decides to Remain on the Defensive—He makes Preparations and Selects a Position for a Decisive Battle.

(2) The Allies Remain in Position near Olmütz—Friction between the Austrian and Russian Officers—The Want of Supplies makes Action Necessary—Differences between the Allied Commanders.

(3) The Allies Decide to Attack the French—They Commence their Advance—Bagration Drives back Murat—The Allies Bivouac on the Pratzen Heights—Description of the Battlefield.

(1) On the 21st of November the French force in the neighbourhood of Brünn amounted to about 50,000 men, composed of the bulk of Murat's cavalry, the Guard, and the corps of Soult and Lannes. Mortier's corps, crippled by its losses at Dürrenstein, had been detailed to garrison Vienna, while Bernadotte, who after considerable delay had crossed the Danube at Krems in pursuit of Kutusoff, was ordered to Iglau, in Bohemia, to watch the force which the Archduke Ferdinand was organising to threaten the French communications.

Davout's corps was east of Vienna, between Nikolsburg and Pressburg, observing the hostile detachments in Hungary, while Marmont was near Leoben, in Styria, ready to check the Archduke Charles should he advance on the Austrian capital. Ney was in the Eastern Tyrol, and Massena, the bulk of whose corps was engaged in the siege of Venice, had strong detachments in the mountains of Carniola, near Görze, and at Laibach.

There were, besides, various garrisons at the most important points on the long line of communications, principally furnished by Augereau's corps, which was no longer required in the Tyrol, while at Linz, Klein and Baraguey d'Hilliers' dragoons guarded the important crossing and kept an eye on the Archduke Ferdinand. Napoleon decided to remain at Brünn, which was as far as he could safely venture, for Prussia's attitude was causing him considerable uneasiness and his communications were dangerously extended; consequently, he used all his great diplomatic ability to induce the Allies to attack him, and sent Savary to their head-quarters to open negotiations.

The emperor had so disposed his corps that Davout and Bernadotte could join him in time for the decisive battle, which he hoped would end the campaign before Prussia could make up her mind to intervene. As usual, he made most careful preparations for every possible eventuality; an alternative line of retreat was mapped out north of the Danube as far as Linz, and a second bridge thrown across the river opposite Vienna.

What Napoleon most desired was that the Allies should attack him in his chosen position before they had been joined by the Archduke Charles, and to this end he used every resource of diplomacy. He carefully reconnoitred the country in the vicinity of Brünn, eventually selecting a position behind the Goldbach, a small rivulet some six miles east of Brünn, on the road to Olmütz, in which to await attack.

(2) After effecting their junction at Wischau on the 18th of November, the Allies, some 80,000 strong, continued their retreat, eventually going into camp at Olshan, a few miles southwest of Olmütz, and leaving a line of outposts at Prosnitz, on the road to Brünn. Both Russian contingents were completely exhausted; Kutusoff's men had been marching and fighting without intermission for nearly a month, while Buxhowden's corps had been hurried forward by forced marches since they had crossed the frontier, in spite of bad roads and inclement weather. Prince John Liechtenstein's corps consisted principally of the recently raised 6th Battalions of the Austrian infantry regiments, which had received barely a month's training, though the bulk

of his cavalry had taken part in the retreat from the Inn.

Time was of vital importance to the Allies, for the Russian Guard and Essen's corps, in all some 20,000 men, had not yet arrived, and the Archduke Charles would be forced by the presence of the French corps round Vienna to make a detour through Hungary, to join the main body of the Allies.

From the commencement of the campaign the friction between the Austrians and the Russians had steadily increased; the former, who had struggled almost single-handed against the French since the outbreak of the Revolutionary Wars, had been by no means eager to embark on a fresh campaign, and bitterly resented the taunts of their allies and the barbarous habits of their troops. The Russians, on the other hand, complained that the campaign had been almost lost in consequence of Mack's incompetence and the shameful way in which the Austrians had surrendered.

Owing to the rapid and totally unexpected retreat, no supply depots had been formed at Olmütz, the surrounding districts were quickly denuded of food and forage, and the Allies were threatened with imminent starvation if they remained much longer in their present position. They had several courses open to them; they could:

(1) Remain in their present position until the arrival of the Archduke Charles;

(2) move southward into Hungary to facilitate their junction with him;

(3) fall back towards the Russian frontier to tap fresh sources of supply;

(4) advance at once to bring Napoleon to action.

The Emperor Alexander, who, in reality, exercised supreme command over the Allied Armies, was eager to try conclusions with his great opponent, while his younger officers, with an overweening belief in their own and their men's courage, clamoured to be led at once against the French. Kutusoff, the nominal *generalissimo*, was strongly in favour of a temporary retreat, but was far too much of a courtier to openly oppose the wishes of the *Czar*. The more experienced of the Russian commanders, Bagration, Miloradovitch, Langeron, Dochtorotf, as well as Liechtenstein, were strongly opposed to attacking the French position, but they were overruled by the younger and more hotheaded officers, who urged that the very fact that Napoleon had opened negotiations showed that he was aware that he was almost at the end of his tether, and clamoured for an immediate attack before he commenced his retreat.

Weyrother, the Austrian quartermaster-general, who was acting as chief of the staff to Kutusoff, alone among the senior officers was in favour of an immediate attack, and, unfortunately for the Allies, he possessed a considerable amount of influence at the Imperial headquarters.

He was responsible for the ill-judged plan which led to the crushing defeat of the Russo-Austrian Army on the field of Austerlitz, and in his eagerness to outmanoeuvre his great opponent, he led the Allies into the trap which Napoleon had so carefully prepared for them. Assuming that the French would passively await attack, and that they were much weaker than was really the case, he intended to turn their right flank, cut them off from Vienna, and drive them northward away from their communications.

On the 2th of November the Russian Guard, a splendid body of men 8,000 strong, under the Grand Duke Constantine, arrived in camp in perfect condition, in spite of the fact that they had covered the entire distance from St. Petersburg by a series of forced marches over almost impassable roads. Though an advance had been decided upon at the Council of War held on the 24th of November, it was not until three days later, after confusion and delay, that the Allies, marching in five columns, left Olshan, arriving at Prosnitz the same evening.

On the 28th their advance guard, under Bagration, drove Murat from Wischau, the latter, who had been ordered not to offer a prolonged resistance, falling back to the Pratzen Heights, in front of the previously selected position. Napoleon, who had witnessed the skirmish, saw with immense satisfaction that the

GENERAL JOACHIM-NAPOLÉON MURAT,
FRENCH MARSHAL

Allies were advancing in earnest, and during the evening sent orders to Bernadotte and Davout to join him.

Arriving at Wischau on the 29th of November, Kutusoff abandoned the main road to Brünn and moved southward to bring the bulk of his force opposite his opponent's right flank. Napoleon withdrew Soult's corps to the main position behind the Goldbach, leaving only a screen, under Murat, on the high ground round Pratzen. Kutusoff reached Butschowitz, within fifteen miles of the French position, on the 30th, and then wheeled his columns to the right, marching towards the heights situated in the angle between the Goldbach and the Littawa streams.

On the 1st of December he occupied the Pratzen Ridge, from which Murat had retired, and his advanced troops skirmished throughout the day with the French outposts. Bagration's column bivouacked north of the main road from Olmütz to Brünn, close to Rausnitz, the remaining columns moving into position on his left, the bulk of the main body being located on the high ground south of Pratzen village opposite the French centre.

Carefully observing the Allies' movements, Napoleon noticed with delight they were following the course he had anticipated, and evidently intended to operate against his right flank. He had thoroughly reconnoitred his chosen battlefield, and had selected a strong point on which to rest his left flank, an isolated hill north of the main road a little distance in front of the Goldbach, which, from its resemblance to a conical hill near Alexandria, had been christened Santon by the veterans of the Egyptian Campaign.

He had carefully superintended its fortification and allotted it a special garrison under Claparède. From the "Santon" the position extended southward across the Brünn-Olmütz road behind the Goldbach to the lower ground, which was intersected by ponds, and the right, which was refused, was covered by the Satschen and Menitz Lakes. Lannes's corps was on the extreme left behind the "Santon" with Murat's cavalry on his right, astride the main road; next came Bernadotte's corps, extending as far south as the village of Puntowitz, partly in the valley behind the Goldbach, partly on the high ground west of Girzikowitz.

Soult held the centre with two divisions between Puntow-itz and Kobelnitz, while the remaining division, under Legrand, formed a screen from the latter village to Telnitz, behind the lakes on the extreme right.

The villages of Girzikowitz, Puntowitz, Kobelnitz, Sokolnitz, and Telnitz, covering the crossings over the Goldbach, were held by detachments of infantry, and the frontage of the whole posi-tion, over which the troops were very unequally distributed, was, roughly, about six miles. The left, and more especially the centre, were strongly held, while the right, from Kobelnitz to Telnitz, was only occupied by Legrand's division, but on the day of battle would be strengthened by Davout's two divisions. The reserve, consisting of the Guard and Oudinot's grenadiers, was massed on the high ground south of the main road, in rear of Bernadotte's corps behind the centre, and with this force Napo-leon intended to drive home his decisive counterstroke.

The emperor's plan was extremely simple; foreseeing that the Allies would make their attack against his extreme right, he in-tended to hold them with Legrand and Davout's divisions, and as soon as they were irretrievably committed to their flanking movement, to launch Soult and Bernadotte's corps, supported by the reserve, against their weakened centre on the Pratzen Heights, the key of the position, and cut their army in two.

Lannes and Murat, meanwhile, were to operate vigorously against Bagration, to prevent him sending reinforcements to the critical point. Bernadotte, who had left Wrede's weak Bavarian division at Iglau, arrived on the afternoon of the 1st of Decem-ber, but Davout's two divisions only arrived at Raigern, some five miles in rear of the extreme right of the position, during the night of the 1st of December.

They had made a most arduous march, Friant's Division, from Vienna, having covered ninety miles in forty-eight hours, and in spite of his excellent arrangements, hundreds of weary strag-glers only rejoined their regiments next day, after the battle had actually commenced. Though Davout was one of the ablest and most reliable of the French generals, it was trying his splendid corps to the limit of their endurance to expect them to bear the brunt of the Allies' attack after their exhausting forced march. Gudin's division took no part in the ensuing battle, remaining round Nikolsburg in observation of Merveldt's detached corps.

During the night of the 1st of December, Napoleon was continually on the alert, visiting his troops in their bivouacs and receiving a most enthusiastic reception from the various corps, more especially from the grenadiers, who, twisting the straw of their bedding into torches, caused such an illumination that the Austrians imagined that the French were burning their bivouacs before retreating. The men were eager to fight, longing for a decisive victory which should finish the campaign, hitherto more remarkable for its arduous and continuous marching than for hard fighting. By a singular coincidence, the morrow would be the anniversary of Napoleon's assumption of the title of Emperor, and this fact was hailed as a most favourable omen throughout the army.

CHAPTER 6

The Battle of Austerlitz, 2nd December, 1805

(1) Weyrother's Plan of Attack—Late Issue of Orders—
Advance of the Main Body of the Allies against the French
Right—Davout's Action on the Goldbach.
(2) Napoleon's Counter-stroke against the Hostile Centre—Defeat of the Russian Guard.
(3) The Failure of Bagration's Attack on the French Left—
Rout of the Allies—The Pursuit and the Armistice.

(1) On the evening of the 1st of December, Kienmayer, with
twenty squadrons of Austrian cavalry, five battalions of Light Infantry, and some Cossacks, bivouacked at Aujezd; he was to form
the advance guard of the columns destined to attack the French
right, and was afterwards to cover their outer flank. At midnight
the Allied commanders, with the exception of Bagration, were
summoned to Kutusoff's headquarters at Krenowitz, in rear of
the Pratzen Heights, to receive their orders for the morrow

As soon as they were all assembled, Weyrother read out his
verbose orders for the attack, which were, roughly, as follows:—

1st Column—Lieutenant-General Dochtoroff—24 Russian
Battalions, to march by his left, moving by Aujezd on Telnitz;
after passing Telnitz to move to his right until his leading troops
wore parallel to those of the second column.

2nd Column—Lieutenant-General Langeron—18 Russian
battalions, to move by his left from the Pratzen Heights, cross
the Goldbach between Telnitz and Sokolnitz, and dress on the
first column.

3rd   Column—Lieutenant-General   Prysbyszewsky—18

BIVOUAC ON THE EVE OF THE BATTLE OF AUSTERLITZ

Russian Battalions, to move by his left from the heights north of Pratzen village, cross the Goldbach north of Sokolnitz, near the castle, and then to move forward west of the river as far as the village of Kobelnitz.

4th Column—Lieutenant-General Kolowrat—15 Austrian and 12 Russian battalions to move by his left from his position on the heights in rear of the third column, cross the Goldbach south of Kobelnitz ponds, then move to his right and bring his advanced troops level with the other columns. (The hastily raised Austrian battalions were not at full strength, and the Russians had lost heavily during the retreat front the Ulm.)

5th Column—Lieutenant-General Prince John Liechtenstein—80 Squadrons, to move from the valley east of the heights, behind the position of the third column, towards Blasowitz, and afterwards advance astride of the main road. Kienmayer was to form the advanced guard of the main attack, and afterwards to protect its outer flank.

The original advanced guard, under Prince Bagration—12 Russian battalions and 40 Russian and Austrian squadrons—was to attack the French left, capture the "Santon," and advance straight on Brünn along the main road. The reserve under the Grand Duke Constantine, composed of the Russian Guard, 10 battalions and 18 squadrons, was to move from its position in front of Austerlitz to the heights in rear of Blasowitz to support the right wing. Such was the complicated plan which Weyrother, with incredible folly, had evolved.

Commencing with a march across the front and within easy striking distance of the most resolute and energetic commander of the century, he afterwards intended to force the crossings over the Goldbach, and then, wheeling his four columns to the right, to roll up the French flank, and drive it in on the centre, Bagration and Liechtenstein, meanwhile, were to overthrow the French loft and out them off from Brünn.

His whole scheme rested on the extremely doubtful supposition that his opponent, whose force he had greatly underrated, putting it at 40,000 at the most, would remain passively on the defensive. He had practically no centre, for the Pratzen Heights, the key of the position, would be almost entirely denuded of troops, and as the Grand Duke Constantine was to move up into the first line, he would in reality have no reserve, as well as little connection between his two widely separated attacks. No instructions were given to Buxhowden, who commanded the main attack on the hostile right, in case he was unable to turn the enemy's flank, and the fact that the French might assume the offensive was entirely ignored.

Neither Kutusoff nor Buxhowden made any remark, and Weyrother concluded by saying that he knew the ground well, as he had manoeuvred over it the year before; only Count Bubna, his A.D.C., remarked bluntly that "he hoped he would avoid making the mistakes he had made on that occasion." The allied commanders then departed to join their corps, but so late had the orders been published that the subordinate leaders were unable to get them translated and issue their own orders until after the troops had commenced their march.

The columns commanded by Dochtoroff, Langeron, and Prysbyszewsky quitted their bivouacs at 7 a.m. on the morning of the 2nd of December, but were seriously delayed by the incompetence of the Russian staff officers, who, in many cases, had not yet received their orders. Meanwhile, Kienmayer had attacked the hill east of Telnitz at daybreak, driving the French outposts back after a sharp skirmish, but had been unable to capture the village. However, the leading troops of Dochtoroff's column eventually appeared, and reinforced by some Russian battalions, he managed to drive the weak hostile garrison from the village to the high ground in rear. For some time, the battle raged fiercely in the valley, in spite of the thick mist which enveloped the combatants.

Gradually Dochtoroff deployed the bulk of his column, and as the mist cleared off under the influence of the sun, he made a determined attack, once more capturing Telnitz, which had been retaken by Davout's men, who, marching in haste from Raigern to support Legrand's hard-pressed troops, had seized the village by a vigorous counterattack.

The Battle of Austerlitz, 2nd December, 1805

The French right was forced back to the heights west of the Goldbach, where, however, it resolutely maintained its position.

Soon after 8 a.m. the batteries of the second and third Russian columns, which had been considerably delayed by the cavalry crossing their line of march, opened on Sokolnitz, and an hour later their infantry drove the French from the village to the high ground in rear.

Davout sent Friant to check their advance, and the latter delivered a vigorous counter-stroke, driving them back into the village, which was captured and re-captured several times. Shortly after 10 o'clock the bulk of the second and third columns were deployed for the purpose of making a decisive attack, but were thrown into confusion by the accurate fire of Davout's batteries posted on the high ground west of the stream. Meanwhile, Buxhowden had remained inactive, instead of pressing home an attack with his first column against the French right in rear of Telnitz, which had been considerably weakened by the reinforcements sent to hard-pressed troops round Sokolnitz.

Though the odds against him were nearly four to one, Davout managed to hold his own with the right wing, but it needed all his ability and all his men's dogged courage to check the advance of the powerful Russian columns, supported by their numerous batteries.

NAPOLEON'S COUNTER-STROKE

(2) Though the emperor had been in position early, and had eagerly watched the movements of the hostile troops, he waited patiently for them to irretrievably commit themselves to their turning movement before he launched Soult's Corps, supported by Bernadotte, against the Allies' weakened centre on the Pratzen Heights. Hidden by the mist and the smoke of the bivouac fires, Soult's two divisions were massed in the valley on the eastern bank of the Goldbach; Vandamme was drawn up south of Girzikowitz, with St. Hiliare on his right in front of Puntowitz.

The emperor asked Soult how long it would take for his division to reach the heights, and the marshal replied "Twenty minutes." Shortly after nine o'clock it was reported that the Allies had evacuated the Pratzen Heights, and the emperor ordered Soult to advance; the latter instructed Vandamme to attack north and St. Hiliare to the south of Pratzen, in order to gain possession of the heights as rapidly as possible and to isolate any troops that might be holding the village. The fourth column of the Allies was just moving off in column of route to follow the third, when the French divisions appeared at the western edge of the heights, advancing in two lines, the first extended, and the second, in closer formation, following in support.

At once realising the gravity of the situation, Kutusoff ordered Kolowrat's advance guard to seize Pratzen, while the remainder of his column was to attack St. Hiliare, and Miloradovitch, with some Russian battalions, was to oppose Vandamme. Some Austrian regiments from Kolowrat's second line formed up south of Pratzen, supported by their artillery in position on the heights above Krenowitz, while the remainder of the column, moving to a flank in column of companies, wheeling into line, made a determined attack on St. Hiliare's division.

They were, however, thrown into confusion by an unexpected salvo of grape from nine guns which had accompanied the French advance, and after a stubborn resistance, were driven from the heights in disorder. Miloradovitch had, meanwhile, made a gallant attempt to drive back Vandamme, but in spite of his utmost efforts, his men, staggered by several deadly volleys, were finally completely routed by a vigorous bayonet charge, while the battalions, endeavouring to attack the French left, were almost annihilated.

Kaminskoi's Russian Brigade, which formed the rear of Langeron's column, then made a determined attempt against St. Hiliare's right, but were hurled back after a furious struggle, and the Allies retired altogether from the southern portion of the Pratzen plateau. Meanwhile, a division of Bernadotte's Corps had appeared on Vandamme's left, advancing into the space left vacant by Liechtenstein when he moved his cavalry from Blasowitz to support Bagration.

Vandamme was now ordered to wheel to the right to co-operate with St. Hiliare in an attack on the flanks of the second and

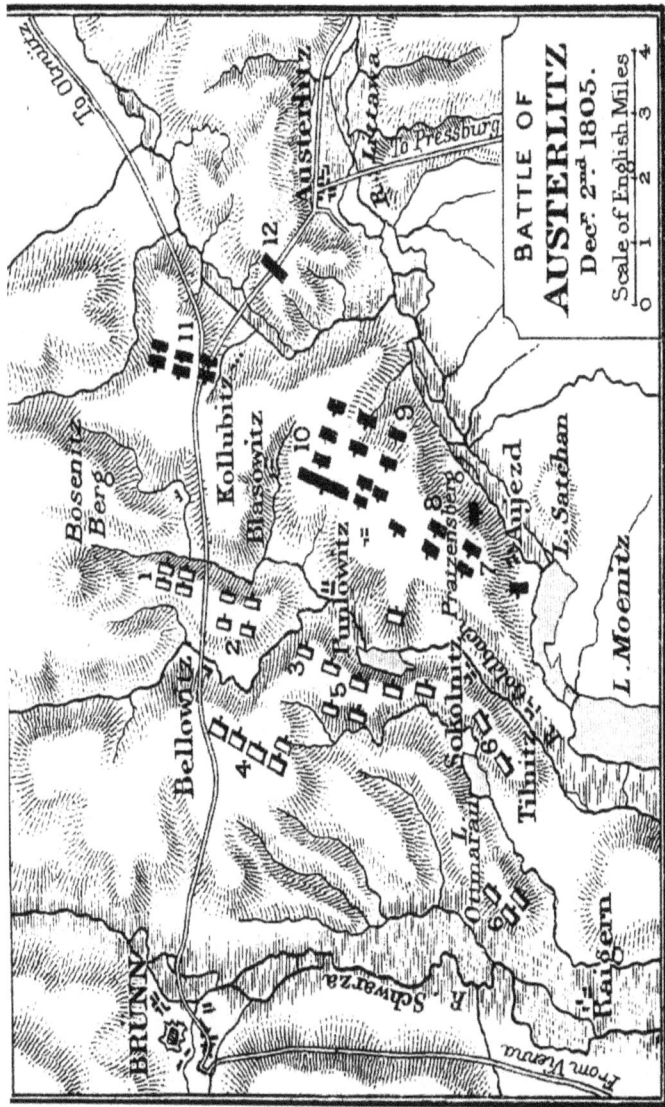

BATTLE OF
AUSTERLITZ
Dec.r 2.nd 1805.

Scale of English Miles
0 1 2 3 4

French. 90,000.
1, Lannes. 2, Bernadotte.
3, Oudinot. Murat. 4, Imp.l Guard under Bessières
5, Soult. 6, Davoust.

Russians & Austrians, 80,000.
7, Doctoroff. 8, Langeron.
9, Prsybyszweski. 10, Milcradowich.
11, Bagration. 12, G.d Duke Constantine.

BRUNN

Bösenitz Berg

Bellowitz

Kollubitz

Blasowitz

Kiritein

Turas

To Olmütz

Austerlitz

R. Littawa

To Pressburg

Sokolnitz

Praczenberg

Aujezd

L. Satchan

L. Moenitz

Raigern

From Vienna

R. Schwarza

Tilnitz

third Russian columns, which were engaged in a fierce struggle with the French round Sokolnitz. Aided by a strong counterstroke made by Legrand's Division from Kobelnitz, they furiously assailed the flank and rear of the two Russian columns, throwing them into confusion and hemming them in between Sokolnitz, Aujezd and the lakes.

The Grand Duke Constantine, who had advanced towards the gap in the line caused by Liechtenstein's withdrawal from Blasowitz, seeing the disaster which had occurred in the centre, moved the Guard to their left in the direction of Pratzen. Falling upon a brigade which Vandamme had detached to guard his left flank, the Russian infantry drove the hostile skirmishers back at the point of the bayonet, while their Horse Guards, overthrowing the opposing cavalry, also furiously attacked the French Brigade.

The latter, taken entirely by surprise, were unable to form square, and the 4th. Regiment were ridden down and cut to pieces, even losing their Eagle in the confusion. The emperor, who was close at hand, noting the disorder into which the infantry had been thrown, ordered Rapp to charge with part of the Guard Cavalry, and Bessières to support him with the remainder.

Charging home at full gallop, Rapp drove the Russian horsemen back past Bernadotte's leading division on to their own infantry, but their second line, composed of the famous Chevalier Guard and Cossacks, fell on the French squadrons, and after a desperate hand-to-hand combat, drove them back. The Russians, however, were furiously attacked by Bessières, at the head of the Horse Grenadiers, and *Chasseurs* of the Guard, and a wild *mêlée* ensued, but nothing could stop the French horsemen, and after a dogged resistance the Russians were driven from the field.

Bernadotte's Divisions, meanwhile, coming up at the double, fell on the infantry of the Russian Guard with the bayonet and totally overthrew them. The Allies' centre was now irretrievably shattered and forced back in wild disorder beyond Krenowitz.

(3) It was a little after one o'clock when Napoleon, seeing

that the battle on the Pratzen Heights had been won, brought forward his reserve, consisting of the Guard Infantry and Oudinot's grenadiers, and posted them on the high ground north of Aujezd to co-operate in the attack on the hostile left, A brigade from Dochtoroff's Column, which had at last been sent by Buxhowden to help the stricken centre, attempted to attack St. Hiliare's division, but, taken in flank by Vandamme was driven from Aujezd with a loss of some 3,000 prisoners and all their guns.

The Allies' left was now in a hopeless position, for Davout, assuming the offensive, drove the Russians out of Menitz after a prolonged and sanguinary struggle, while Legrand and Friant, aided by Oudinot's grenadiers, in a fiercely-contested combat completely routed Prysbyszewsky's men, who, ignorant of the disaster in the centre, were marching towards Kobelnitz in the hopes of joining Kolowrat's column.

At first Buxhowden hoped to defeat the French west of Telnitz, but the ever-increasing pressure on his flank and rear, as well as the overthrow of the bulk of Langeron's column near Sokolnitz, forced him to retire. Calling in Kienmayer's cavalry, and leaving a rear-guard in Telnitz to cover his retreat, Dochtoroff moved towards Aujezd, but, attacked in flank by St. Hiliare, headed off by Vandamme, and pounded by the Guard Artillery, he was forced to abandon his attempt, and the broken remnants of his column fell back in confusion on both sides of Lake Satschen.

Crowded against the lake, the unfortunate Russians, who had lost all formation and were wedged together in a struggling mass, suffered prodigiously from the French artillery. The Russian rear-guard held out heroically in Telnitz, but the village was eventually taken at the point of the bayonet, after a prolonged struggle. Kienmayer, with his Austrian squadrons, protected Dochtoroff's retreat with the most devoted gallantry, charging whenever he found an opportunity, and keeping his force together until the end of the day, when he took up a line of outposts and still retained touch with the victors.

The bulk of the Allies, including the whole of their left wing, fell back in a south-easterly direction, through Ollnitz, towards

Göding, in Hungary.

While these decisive events were taking place on the Pratzen Heights and further to the south, Bagration was fighting a separate battle against Murat and Lannes north of the Olmütz—Brünn road. His task had been to capture the "Santon," drive in the French left and cut them off from Brünn, but he did not receive his orders until about eight o'clock on the morning of the battle, and when he read them he remarked to his staff, "We shall lose the battle." He advanced with his infantry formed in two lines, astride the main road, with a body of cavalry on other flank and in reserve, but had made little progress before he was driven back by Lannes, who had come into action with Suchet's division on the left and Caffarelli's on the right.

Liechtenstein, who had brought his cavalry up on Bagration's inner flank, drove back Kellermann's light cavalry, who wore covering the French advance, but his Russian lancers were thrown into confusion by the deadly fire of Caffarelli's division, which had been formed into squares. Suchet, pushing forward with his division on the extreme left, drove back the Russian infantry, while on the other flank Liechtenstein, who had at last completed his formation, was charged and driven back by Nansouty's heavy cavalry. The Austrian squadrons were again rallied and led against Caffarelli's division, but were beaten off by the deadly fire of the French squares, and eventually driven from the field, completely routed by several brilliant charges delivered by Nansouty's cavalry.

Suchet and Caffarelli then continued their advance, the former against the extreme right of the hostile line and the latter along the main road, forcing Bagration, in spite of a stout resistance, to fall back and reform his line some distance in rear, with his left resting on the main road.

It was only by sheer hard fighting that Bagration managed to hold out till nightfall, when he withdrew in tolerable order to Austerlitz, where he joined some remnants of the Russian Guard.

Napoleon's carefully prepared plans had been completely successful, and his arrangements had been carried out without a hitch; in fact, Austerlitz is one of the most perfect specimens of a battle absolutely fulfilling the intentions of a commander, and had Bernadotte pushed on after defeating the infantry of the Russian Guard, instead of falling back to his original position, the hostile centre would have been annihilated.

The French losses were officially returned at 8,000, but were probably considerably higher, whilst the Russian casualties amounted to 21,000, including 15,000 prisoners (many of whom were wounded), and 130 guns, besides which the Austrians lost over 6,000 killed and wounded and nearly all their artillery.

The various authorities differ considerably as to strength of the opposing armies engaged at Austerlitz, but allowing for the losses sustained during the campaign, Napoleon had probably from sixty to sixty-five thousand men in position and the Allies between eighty-five and ninety thousand troops actually on the field.

A Russian Corps, 12,000 strong, under Essen, was unable to arrive in time to take part in the battle, though their leader, finding it impossible to bring his men into action, pushed forward alone and fell fighting gallantly at the head of Bagration's Squadrons.

CHAPTER 7

The Operations in Northern Italy and the Tyrol

(1) The Role of Massena's Corps—The Archduke Remains on the Defensive—The French Advance—The Battle of Caldiero—Retreat of the Austrians—Rearguard Actions—The Archduke Decides to Abandon Italy. (2) The Austrians Ordered to Evacuate the Tyrol—Ney Advances and Occupies Innsbruck—Fate of the Austrian Detachments—The Archdukes Unite their Forces and Move into Hungary.

(1) Napoleon was fully aware that the army in Italy would be numerically inferior to that of the Allies, and that he would have to deal with an Anglo-Russian Expedition, which would probably land at Naples.

However, he relied on Massena, one of his most trusted lieutenants, to contain the Archduke Charles until his own operations in the Valley of the Danube had produced their effect, and he considered that St, Cyr, with some 20,000 men, would be able to deal with the Allies in Southern Italy.

In spite of the Vice-Roi Eugene's exertions, Massena found on his arrival on the 8th of September, that the force assembling on the upper Chiese, in front of Brescia, amounted to little over 30,000 men.

The marshal was instructed to concentrate his force as rapidly as possible in front of Peschiera, covered by the Adige; his left was to rest on the strong position of Rivoli, in front of Lake Garda, his right on the fortress of Verona, and his cavalry and light troops were to watch the line of the Adige as far as Leg-

107

nano. He was instructed to maintain himself in this formidable position until the progress of events in the main theatre of operations forced his opponent to retire.

Owing to the reinforcements sent to the Iller, the Archduke Charles found the army assembled on the upper Adige under 90,000 strong, of whom 18,000, under Hiller, were in the Southern Tyrol between Bozen and Trent, and the remainder on the eastern bank of the Adige, between the latter town and Verona. He had originally intended to assume the offensive with about 140,000 men, but several regiments had been diverted to the Iller, and Hiller's corps was ordered to operate in the Tyrol.

Thoroughly realising Mack's incompetence, the archduke, who strongly disapproved of the Allies' plan of campaign, was convinced that he would shortly have to transport his army into the valley of the Danube to check the French advance on Vienna; moreover, he greatly overestimated Massena's force, which he quite erroneously imagined to amount to some 75,000 men. Taking these facts into consideration, and carefully weighing the situation, he decided to remain on the defensive, reasoning that any minor successes he might obtain in northern Italy would be valueless, and decided to keep his army well in hand, so as to be able to transfer it instantly to the main theatre of operations in the valley of the Danube.

By the 26th of September, the date on which Napoleon crossed the Danube, Massena's force, including the garrisons of the fortresses of Peschiera, Verona and Mantua, amounted to some 50,000 men, of whom 40,000 were available for operations in the field.

To enable him to manoeuvre on either bank of the river, Massena seized the bridge over the Adige, opposite Verona, on the night of the 18th of October, driving back the weak Austrian detachment and constructing a bridge head on the eastern bank of the river.

The archduke, who did not intend to dispute the passage of the Adige, had meanwhile concentrated his main body round Caldiero, a naturally strong position some twelve miles from Verona.

On the night of the 24th of October, he received tidings of the Capitulation of Ulm, and keeping the news of the disaster from his army, he immediately commenced to make preparations for retreat.

Owing to the hostility of the inhabitants of the Tyrol, Massena did not hear of Napoleon's success until four days later, but his preparations were so far completed that he was able to advance almost at once. On the 29th of October he crossed the Adige with 35,000 men, driving back the weak Austrian detachments guarding the river, the latter, after a slight resistance, falling back to join the archduke, who had concentrated 45,000 men round Caldiero. The position in which he meant to check the French, before commencing his retreat, was a remarkably strong one; the right rested on the mountains and the left on the marshes bordering the Adige; moreover, it had been carefully strengthened by the construction of redoubts and entrenchments.

In spite of a dense fog, Massena advanced on the 30th of October, sending a strong column, under Verdier, across the Adige below the hostile position, to turn his opponent's left flank, but the column lost its way in the fog, and, making a frontal attack, the battle became general along the whole of the strongly held position.

Both sides fought with the greatest gallantry throughout the day, but though the French managed to retain possession of the town, they entirely failed to effect a lodgement in the main position.

Next morning Massena again attacked, but without much result, while the archduke, determined to cripple his assailant before commencing his retreat, launched several vigorous counter-strokes against the French flanks. He succeeded in throwing them on the defensive, and at daybreak the next morning, the 1st of November, his main body commenced to retire in three columns, leaving a small rear-guard to hold the position and cover their retreat. The latter held their ground for twenty-four hours before falling back to Vicenza, where the archduke had left a detachment to cover their retreat and enable them to cross the river.

Massena's pursuit was temporarily checked, as his field guns were powerless against the walls of the town, and by the time his heavy artillery arrived the Austrians, evacuating Vicenza and leaving their wounded behind them, had continued their retreat.

Their main body, meanwhile, had crossed the Brenta, and leaving a rear-guard on the river to check the enemy's advance, continued their march towards the Piave.

This was successfully accomplished by the rear-guard, though it suffered heavily, but its gallant stand enabled the three columns of the main body to concentrate behind the Tagliamento on the 9th of November without molestation.

The archduke, seriously alarmed by the news of Napoleon's rapid progress towards Vienna, made up his mind to entirely abandon Italy, and to endeavour to effect his junction with the main army of the Allies, but he also intended to check the pursuit as long as possible by leaving detachments to dispute the passage of the Tagliamento and Isonzo.

Halting for a few days at Prewald, he eventually marched northward to the Drave to join the Archduke John, who was retreating from the Tyrol,

Massena, meanwhile, who had been delayed by the detachments left at the various rivers, abandoned his pursuit as soon as he realised that his opponent had definitely left Italy.

As he was anxious to obtain news of Ney's movements in the Tyrol, he sent a detachment to Villach while he occupied himself with the siege of Venice; he also stationed a couple of small columns in Carniola to keep touch with a body of Austrian troops under Bellegarde who had been left to watch the French by the archduke.

(2) At the commencement of the campaign, the Austrian force in the Tyrol consisted of about 30,000 Regular troops and the local militia, but as soon as it was evident that the decisive operations would take place in the valley of the Danube, Mack ordered some 15,000 men to join him on the Iller. Auffenberg's column, originally about 8,000 strong, was scattered by Murat at Wertingen on the 8th of October, while Jellachich, after reaching Ulm, was ordered to return *via* Memmingen, but the

town had meanwhile surrendered to Soult, and it was with the greatest difficulty that he managed to escape into the Tyrol with some 6,000 men.

Shortly before the Capitulation of Ulm, the Archduke John arrived in the Tyrol, and, calling up Hiller's corps from Trent, he endeavoured to organise a scheme of defence; he had hardly commenced operations, however, when, in consequence of Kutusoff's retreat, he was ordered to evacuate the Tyrol and leave its defence to the local militia.

He ordered a general concentration at Innsbruck, intending to fall back *via* Radstadt to join the Russians in opposing the French advance on Vienna, but his flank guard was driven in by the Bavarians, and he was forced to move southward through the Brenner Pass. A day or two later Deroi's Bavarian division, which was advancing from the valley of the Danube to co-operate in the invasion of the Tyrol, was repulsed by the local Militia and compelled to retire to Salzburg.

Meanwhile, Ney's corps had been practically broken up, Dupont's division had followed the main body and was eventually incorporated in the new corps commanded by Mortier, Loisson's division and the cavalry remained to guard the prisoners; consequently, when the marshal marched from Ulm on the 27th of October, he found himself at the head of little over 8,000 men.

He met with no opposition during his advance until he reached the lines of Scharnitz, which he carried by assault on the 4th of November, and entered Innsbruck unopposed next day.

The position of the Austrian detachments was rapidly becoming critical, for Augereau, crossing the Rhine at Huningen, north of Basle, towards the end of October, had advanced into the Voralberg, the north-western district of the Tyrol. The archduke managed to join Hiller at the Brenner Pass, after which he continued his retreat to Brixen, where he hoped to effect his junction with the detachments under Rohan and Jellachich.

Ney waited in Innsbruck five days for the Bavarians, then continued his march southward on the 10th of November, but was checked on the following day by the Austrian rear-guard at Stafflack.

As the Archduke John could hear nothing of his other detachments, he resumed his retreat through Villach to Klagenfurt, which place he reached on the 20th of November. Here he halted for a couple of days and then continued his march towards the Drave, effecting his junction with his brother, the Archduke Charles, near Marburg on the 26th of November.

Ney continued his pursuit as far as Brixen, but was unable to come up with the Austrians or prevent the junction of their forces, and remained in the eastern Tyrol, endeavouring to open up communication with Massena in Italy and Marmont in Styria.

Meanwhile Jellachich, who had remained too long in the Voralberg, attempted to retreat, but was surrounded by Augereau's corps at Hohenembs and forced to surrender, only a few of his squadrons succeeding in escaping across the French communications into Bohemia.

Rohan, finding himself unable to join the Archduke John, made a gallant attempt to escape into Italy with his column, which amounted to about 6,000 men. Marching southward, he drove the small French garrison from Bozen, and moving *via* Trent into Venetia, he recaptured Bassano on the 23rd of November, but was surrounded next day by St. Cyr's troops at Castlefranco and forced to lay down his arms.

The Austrian forces on the Drave now amounted to about 80,000 men, and the Archduke Charles originally intended to march to Vienna; but hearing that the French had occupied the city, he decided to march through Hungary to join the main body of the Allies in Moravia.

However, soon after reaching Komorn, on the Danube, he received news of their disastrous defeat at Austerlitz, and of the subsequent armistice.

Throughout the campaign the Archduke Charles had been paralyzed by the faulty strategy of the Allies, of which he thoroughly disapproved, and his great talents had been entirely wasted; his knowledge of Mack's incompetence had prevented him making use of his numerical superiority in Italy, but he had conducted his retreat in face of his able opponent with the greatest skill. The Austrian force in the Tyrol had been absolutely useless, but it had been so reduced by the large reinforcements sent to Mack, that in any case it could have exercised little influence on the campaign.

After his escape from Ulm at the end of October, the Archduke Ferdinand had collected some 15,000 men in Bohemia, with the intention of acting against the French communications, but the presence of Bernadotte's corps at Iglau had prevented him accomplishing anything.

As soon as that marshal was withdrawn to take part in the Battle of Austerlitz, the archduke advanced, and after a sharp conflict forced Wrede's weak Bavarian Division to retire, but his action led to no result, as by that time the main army of the Allies had been defeated and the armistice concluded.

The Chronology of the Campaign of 1805

August

70,000 Austrians, under the Archduke Ferdinand, concentrate at Wels on the Traun.

24th. Napoleon makes a secret Treaty with the Elector of Bavaria.

25th. The 1st Russian Contingent enters Galicia.

26th. Nansouty's cavalry despatched to the Rhine.

28th. The French commence their march to the Rhine.

30th. Murat appointed Lieutenant-General of the Empire and ordered to superintend the concentration of the French Corps.

September

4th. The Austrians advance from Wels

8th. Cross the Inn and enter Bavaria.

11th. Occupy Munich, the Bavarian Amy escape northward.

18th. The Austrians reach the line of the Iller.

20th. They occupy Ulm.

23rd. The French Corps commence to arrive on the Rhine. Marmont reaches Mayence. Kienmayer ordered to Ingolstadt.

25th. Murat, supported by Lannes, advances through the Black Forest to screen the advance of the main body.

26th. The French Corps commence crossing the Rhine.

27th. Bernadotte reaches Wurzburg.

October

2nd. The French Army reaches the line Stuttgart-Wurzburg, Bavarians at Bamberg.

5th. Mack endeavours to concentrate at Ulm and Günzburg. The French centre is round Nördlingen.

6th. The French advance to the line Heidenheim-Eichstadt. Kienmayer retreats to the southern bank of the Danube.

7th. Mack decides to fall on the heads of the French Corps as they cross the Danube.

Auffenberg ordered to Wertingen. Murat, Soult and the Guard cross the river.

8th. Murat defeats Auffenberg at Wertingen. Lannes, Marmont and Davout cross the Danube.

9th. Bernadotte crosses at Ingolstadt. Mack abandons his march to Augsburg and decides to retreat north of the Danube.

Ney seizes the bridges at Günzburg. Napoleon orders Murat, with Ney and Lannes, to advance on Ulm, and Soult to Landsberg.

11th. Dupont checks the Austrian attempt to retreat at Haslach.

13th. Mack again attempts to retreat, marching out of Ulm in two columns. Napoleon determines to prevent his retreat north of the Danube.

14th. Ney forces the bridge at Elchingen and drives the Austrians back into Ulm. Soult captures Memmingen.

15th. Ney captures the Michelsberg and drives the Austrians into Ulm.

16th. Murat pursues Werneck. Ulm bombarded.

17th. Mack agrees to surrender unless relieved before the 25th.

18th. Werneck surrenders near Nördlingen.

19th. The last Russian column arrives on the Inn (the first arrived on the 11th).

20th. Mack surrenders with 30,000 men, Murat halts at

Nuremberg.

23rd. Kutusoff hears of the Capitulation of Ulm.

25th. Napoleon concentrates his corps round Munich.

26th. The French advance towards the Inn. Kutusoff commences his retreat to join the Second Russian Contingent.

28th. The French cross the Inn.

30th. Murat drives the Russian rear-guard from Ried.

31st. Overtakes them again and drives them from Lambach.

November

3rd. The Russians abandon the line of the Enns.

4th. Skirmish with the hostile rear-guards at Enns and Steyer.

5th. Bagration checks the French pursuit at Amstetten.

7th. Murat occupies Mölk.

8th. Kutusoff halts on the St. Pölten Ridge. Davout defeats Merveldt at Mariazell.

9th. Kutusoff crosses the Danube at Krems and burns the bridge.

11th. The Russians defeat Mortier at Dürrenstein. Murat ordered to halt.

12th. Murat ordered to occupy Vienna.

13th. Murat seizes the Florisdörf bridge opposite Vienna,

14th. Murat, Soult and Lannes sent in pursuit of the Russians *via* Stockerau, while Bernadotte and Mortier follow them from Krems.

15th. Murat comes up with the Russian flank guard, under Bagration, near Hollabrünn, and negotiates while the Russian main body slips away.

16th. Bagration fights a successful rear-guard action north of Hollabrünn.

17th. The French occupy Zniam.

18th. Kutusoff effects his junction with Buxhowden at Wischau and continues his retreat. Bagration rejoins the main body.

19th. Murat occupies Brünn.

20th. Napoleon arrives and establishes his headquarters at Brünn.

21st. Cavalry skirmish at Rausnitz.

22nd. The Allies go into camp at Olschan, a few miles from Olmütz.

24th. Council of War decide on attacking the French immediately.

25th. The Grand Duke Constantine arrives with the Russian Guard.

27th. The Allies commence their advance towards Brünn.

28th. Bagration drives back Murat, the Allies reach Wischau. Napoleon calls in Bernadotte and Davout.

29th. The French retire behind the Goldbach, the Allies move southward to Butsohowitz.

30th. The Allies move west to Austerlitz.

December

1st. The Allies occupy the Pratzen Heights. Bernadotte's Corps arrives, Davout reaches Raigern (five miles from the position).

2nd. The Battle of Austerlitz.

3rd. Pursuit of the Allies.

4th. The Armistice.

EVENTS IN NORTHERN ITALY AND THE TYROL.

September

8th, Massena assumes command of the French troops in Italy.

26th. The French concentrate north of Verona.

October

8th. Jellachich ordered from Stockach to Ulm.

16th. He returns to the Voralberg (N.W. Tyrol).

18th. The French seize the bridge over the Adige at Verona.

24th. The Archduke Charles hears of the Capitulation of Ulm and determines to retreat after checking the French at Caldiero.

27th. Ney marches from Ulm to subdue the Tyrol.

28th. Massena hears of the Capitulation of Ulm.

29th. He commences his advance. The Archduke John ordered to evacuate the Tyrol.

30th. The French attack the Austrian position at Caldiero.

31st. Massena again attacks the position without success. The Bavarians attack the Austrians in the Tyrol and force them to retreat southward instead of joining the Russians in the Valley of the Danube.

November

1st. The Archduke Charles retreats from Caldiero,

2nd. The Bavarians repulsed by the Tyrolese at Scharnitz.

4th. Ney storms the lines of Scharnitz.

5th. The French enter Innsbruck.

7th, The Archduke Charles crosses the Tagliamento.

8th. The Archduke John joins Hiller at the Brenner Pass.

10th. Ney advances southward from Innsbruck.

11th. He is checked by the Austrian rear-guard at Stafflack.

13th. The Archduke John continues his retreat.

14th. Jellachich is surrounded by Hohenembs and forced to surrender to Augereau.

16th. The Archduke Charles entirely abandons Northern Italy.

20th. The Archduke John retires to Klagenfurt.

24th. Rohan, who has escaped from the Tyrol into Italy, is surrounded near Bassano and forced to surrender to St. Cyr.

26th. The archdukes effect their junction near Marburg on the Drave. They decide to march through Hungary to join the main body of the Allies in Moravia.

December

6th. They reach Komorn on the Danube and hear of the Armistice.

Appendix

On a war footing, the strength of the corps varied from 25,000 to 40,000 men.

Each corps was composed of two, three or four divisions.

The division consisted of two brigades, each containing two regiments.

The regiment was composed of three battalions, the first and second being "Service Battalions," and the third a Depot Battalion; the latter remained in France, received the recruits for training and furnished the necessary drafts to keep the "Service Battalions" up to strength.

There were nine companies in the battalion, including "light" and "grenadier" companies, though the latter were often detached from their regiments and formed into a separate corps, as in the case of Oudinot's command.

At war strength, the company, including all ranks, numbered 140 effectives, so that at the commencement of the campaign the battalion took the field about 1,100 or 1,200 strong.

Two batteries were attached to each infantry division.

The corps troops consisted of three or four regiments of light cavalry, an artillery park with one or two batteries attached, a detachment of engineers and details belonging to the military train and pay department.

The cavalry regiments consisted of three or four squadrons, each sub-divided into two companies of a hundred sabres.

The whole of the mounted troops, with the exception of the regiments allotted to the infantry divisions, were formed into an independent corps, styled the Reserve Cavalry, under a selected commander.

LEONAUR

ALSO FROM LEONAUR
AVAILABLE IN SOFTCOVER OR HARDCOVER WITH DUST JACKET

THE FALL OF THE MOGHUL EMPIRE OF HINDUSTAN *by H. G. Keene*—By the beginning of the nineteenth century, as British and Indian armies under Lake and Wellesley dominated the scene, a little over half a century of conflict brought the Moghul Empire to its knees.

LADY SALE'S AFGHANISTAN *by Florentia Sale*—An Indomitable Victorian Lady's Account of the Retreat from Kabul During the First Afghan War.

THE CAMPAIGN OF MAGENTA AND SOLFERINO 1859 *by Harold Carmichael Wylly*—The Decisive Conflict for the Unification of Italy.

FRENCH'S CAVALRY CAMPAIGN *by J. G. Maydon*—A Special Correspondent's View of British Army Mounted Troops During the Boer War.

CAVALRY AT WATERLOO *by Sir Evelyn Wood*—British Mounted Troops During the Campaign of 1815.

THE SUBALTERN *by George Robert Gleig*—The Experiences of an Officer of the 85th Light Infantry During the Peninsular War.

NAPOLEON AT BAY, 1814 *by F. Loraine Petre*—The Campaigns to the Fall of the First Empire.

NAPOLEON AND THE CAMPAIGN OF 1806 *by Colonel Vachée*—The Napoleonic Method of Organisation and Command to the Battles of Jena & Auerstädt.

THE COMPLETE ADVENTURES IN THE CONNAUGHT RANGERS *by William Grattan*—The 88th Regiment during the Napoleonic Wars by a Serving Officer.

BUGLER AND OFFICER OF THE RIFLES *by William Green & Harry Smith*—With the 95th (Rifles) during the Peninsular & Waterloo Campaigns of the Napoleonic Wars.

NAPOLEONIC WAR STORIES *by Sir Arthur Quiller-Couch*—Tales of soldiers, spies, battles & sieges from the Peninsular & Waterloo campaingns.

CAPTAIN OF THE 95TH (RIFLES) *by Jonathan Leach*—An officer of Wellington's sharpshooters during the Peninsular, South of France and Waterloo campaigns of the Napoleonic wars.

RIFLEMAN COSTELLO *by Edward Costello*—The adventures of a soldier of the 95th (Rifles) in the Peninsular & Waterloo Campaigns of the Napoleonic wars.

LEONAUR

ALSO FROM LEONAUR
AVAILABLE IN SOFTCOVER OR HARDCOVER WITH DUST JACKET

OFFICERS & GENTLEMEN *by Peter Hawker & William Graham*—Two Accounts of British Officers During the Peninsula War: Officer of Light Dragoons by Peter Hawker & Campaign in Portugal and Spain by William Graham .

THE WALCHEREN EXPEDITION *by Anonymous*—The Experiences of a British Officer of the 81st Regt. During the Campaign in the Low Countries of 1809.

LADIES OF WATERLOO *by Charlotte A. Eaton, Magdalene de Lancey & Juana Smith*—The Experiences of Three Women During the Campaign of 1815: Waterloo Days by Charlotte A. Eaton, A Week at Waterloo by Magdalene de Lancey & Juana's Story by Juana Smith.

JOURNAL OF AN OFFICER IN THE KING'S GERMAN LEGION *by John Frederick Hering*—Recollections of Campaigning During the Napoleonic Wars.

JOURNAL OF AN ARMY SURGEON IN THE PENINSULAR WAR *by Charles Boutflower*—The Recollections of a British Army Medical Man on Campaign During the Napoleonic Wars.

ON CAMPAIGN WITH MOORE AND WELLINGTON *by Anthony Hamilton*—The Experiences of a Soldier of the 43rd Regiment During the Peninsular War.

THE ROAD TO AUSTERLITZ *by R. G. Burton*—Napoleon's Campaign of 1805.

SOLDIERS OF NAPOLEON *by A. J. Doisy De Villargennes & Arthur Chuquet*—The Experiences of the Men of the French First Empire: Under the Eagles by A. J. Doisy De Villargennes & Voices of 1812 by Arthur Chuquet .

INVASION OF FRANCE, 1814 *by F. W. O. Maycock*—The Final Battles of the Napoleonic First Empire.

LEIPZIG—A CONFLICT OF TITANS *by Frederic Shoberl*—A Personal Experience of the 'Battle of the Nations' During the Napoleonic Wars, October 14th-19th, 1813.

SLASHERS *by Charles Cadell*—The Campaigns of the 28th Regiment of Foot During the Napoleonic Wars by a Serving Officer.

BATTLE IMPERIAL *by Charles William Vane*—The Campaigns in Germany & France for the Defeat of Napoleon 1813-1814.

SWIFT & BOLD *by Gibbes Rigaud*—The 60th Rifles During the Peninsula War.

www.ingramcontent.com/pod-product-compliance
Lightning Source LLC
Chambersburg PA
CBHW031900090426
42741CB00005B/577